"*The Gift of Friendship* came to me exactly one year after an out-of-state move. With the power and importance of human connection high on my radar, I found myself nodding, laughing, and wiping away tears with each page-turn. The beautifully crafted stories in this book reveal exactly what I've found to be true: friendship can be flawed but still provide perfect healing. Friendship can be stretched by time and distance but still come back unscathed. Friendship can be brief but still have a lifelong impact. Friendship can be completely unexpected but still divinely planned. This lovely book reminds us that time with friends is healing time; it is holy time. And no matter how busy we are or how much we have going on, we must make time for one of life's greatest blessings."

—**Rachel Macy Stafford**, *New York Times* bestselling author of *Hands Free Mama*

"In a culture that glorifies busy, *The Gift of Friendship* is a refreshing reminder of the importance of investing in relationships that fulfill the soul. This uplifting collection of stories invites you to settle in and rediscover why friendship truly is a gift. Its beautiful photographs and encouraging words make it the perfect gift (no pun intended!) for the girlfriends in your life."

—**Kayla Aimee**, author of *Anchored: Finding Hope in the Unexpected*

"Reading this book is like spending time with a group of encouraging friends. It's full of laughter and tears, beauty and brokenness, inspiration and honesty. Dawn Camp has created a warm, welcoming place our hearts can go back to again and again whenever we need to remember we're not alone."

—**Holley Gerth**, *Wall Street Journal* bestselling author of *You're Already Amazing*

"I was late to discovering the deep beauty of friendships among women. I moved a lot during my growing up years, and later became busy with work and kids and, well, *life*. I missed out on some of the best moments I could have shared with a friend, simply because I didn't realize my need for it. Fortunately, a couple of friends stuck with me as I found my way, and I've come to know just how very much I *do* need them. As a 'beginner' in friendships, I find this book particularly meaningful. It makes me appreciate the friends I have and makes me want to reach out and widen my circle even further. It reminds me of the treasures I have all around me: women who enrich my life with their presence and who inspire me to do the same for them. *The Gift of Friendship* is a book you'll want to give to every one of your friends, because you'll see your own friendships in the pages and you'll just *have* to share it!"

—**Rachel Anne Ridge**, artist, blogger, and author of *Flash: The Homeless Donkey Who Taught Me about Life, Faith, and Second Chances*

the gift of friendship

STORIES THAT CELEBRATE
THE BEAUTY OF SHARED MOMENTS

Dawn Camp,
EDITOR & PHOTOGRAPHER

Revell

a division of Baker Publishing Group
Grand Rapids, Michigan

© 2016 by Dawn Camp

Published by Revell
a division of Baker Publishing Group
P.O. Box 6287, Grand Rapids, MI 49516-6287
www.revellbooks.com

Paperback edition published 2017
ISBN 978-0-8007-2397-2

Printed in the United States of America

The Library of Congress has cataloged the previous edition as follows:
The gift of friendship : stories that celebrate the beauty of shared moments / Dawn Camp, editor & photographer.
    pages cm
    ISBN 978-0-8007-2380-4 (cloth)
    1. Christian women—Religious life. 2. Female friendship—religious aspects—Christianity. I. Camp, Dawn, editor.
BV4527.G54 2016
241'.6762082—dc23   2015027810

Published in association with William K. Jensen Literary Agency, 119 Bampton Court, Eugene, Oregon, 97404.

17 18 19 20 21 22 23   7 6 5 4 3 2 1

To ALL,   Dec
                           2019

For my dear friends:
because of you,
I know what true friendship
looks like.

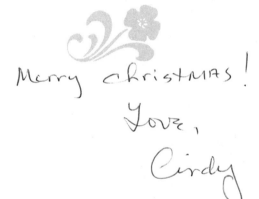

Merry christmas!
Love,
Cindy

contents

foreword

jennifer dukes lee

It was the morning I sat down to begin reading this beautiful book, the one you now hold in your hands. I had read only two pages when my iPhone beeped with a text message. The message came from a woman I had recently met. She took a risk, reaching out to someone she barely knew, by texting me with sixteen words of vulnerability: "I feel so invisible. I need friends. I'm to the point of pretty much giving up."

My heart broke when I read her words, because they are the echo of so many women I've met across the country as an author and speaker. Women want to know they matter. They want to know they're loved. They want to know they're not alone.

I texted back: "Don't give up, friend. You are seen and known. You are not invisible to God. And you are not invisible to me. Believe everything that Jesus says about you—not the least of which is this: He calls you friend."

I prayed for my new friend, and then I returned to the pages of this book to find Dawn's words: "We need our people. We need friends standing in our corner, cheering us on, believing in us. We need listening ears, sharers of inside jokes, keepers of secrets."

Her words were so perfect, so timely. When I read them, I felt tears stinging in the corners of my eyes. Tears of sadness for every woman who's ever felt relationally bankrupt, and tears of joy for all the friends who've poured life into my soul.

The thing is, I have tasted the sweet gift of friendship. My people love me for me. These are women who don't care about my muffin top or my crazy hair, which has its own zip code most mornings. My friends take me as is, despite the fact that I'm forgetful and quirky. Despite the fact that there are, right now, petrified French fries that have been lurking under my car seats since 2013. I am soul-embedded with these women. We've seen each other through cancer, death, job loss, and betrayal.

But I've also felt the sting of loneliness. Several weeks ago, Dawn emailed me to ask if I would write a foreword for this book, a collection of touching stories and gorgeous photographs that highlight the beautiful bond of friendship. She had no idea that I was struggling through my own season of loneliness.

In all my busyness with ministry obligations, I had slowly isolated myself. I had forgotten how much I needed my people. Dawn's book was a timely gift because it reminded me what

I knew deep in my heart but had forgotten: we are better together.

While reading these stories, I vowed to invest in my people— and I vowed to allow people to invest in me again.

I don't know where these words find you today. Maybe you're feeling invisible, like my new friend. This book is a fresh reminder that you are seen and known—that you are not invisible to Jesus, Who calls you friend.

For anyone feeling alone, this book is an invitation to go first, to be the friend you want to have, or perhaps to send sixteen words of vulnerability to a new friend.

Maybe you've been blessed with beautiful friendships, but you desire deeper connection with those heart sisters. Through these stories, you'll hear how women like you have done just that.

Maybe you need to believe again that you—*yes, you!*—have something very special to offer in a friendship.

This book is an invitation and it is also a celebration. A celebration of doing life together, of sticking it out when things get messy, of all the things that make friendships between women so special.

Step inside these pages. Let your heart hear it again. You are known. You are seen. You are not invisible.

Someone out there needs you, friend. Someone needs *the gift of you.*

Jennifer Dukes Lee,
author of *Love Idol*

acknowledgments

$\mathcal{B}$ryan—my husband, my best friend.

My children—Jacob, Hayden, Christian, Sabra, Chloe, Clayton, Felicity, and Lily. I love that children grow into friends.

My sweet friends—I'm humbled by the way you love, support, and pray for me. I wouldn't want to do this without you.

Melissa—thank you for your unconditional friendship, your encouragement, and your words, "It's your time." We all need someone who believes in us.

Michelle—you remind me Who carries me when I'm afraid. And you make me laugh!

Becky—I don't see enough of you, but I know we'll grow old together.

My church gals—have we really been together this long? Thank you for always being here.

My Moe's crowd—food and fellowship are a magical combination. Thank you for the ways you bless my family, one Wednesday night at a time.

Ruth Samsel—more than my agent, my friend.

My Revell team—working with you exceeds expectations. I'm thankful for all you do and I'm so glad we chose each other. You take my work and make it beautiful.

My contributors—I'm thankful for the forty-two writers who shared their words and made this book possible. Your willingness to be vulnerable changes lives.

My family—thank you for how you've loved me through this process. You're the best.

My Savior—thank You for loving me when I'm unlovable; for blessing me exceeding abundantly, above all I could ask or think; and for Your unconditional, saving grace.

introduction

Tentatively emerging from an emotional and spiritual dry spell, the kind that tests both faith and friendships, I pay particular attention to Christian comedian Anita Renfroe's story on the radio on this Sunday morning drive to church. Anita's live performances have a way of breaking down barriers. Laughter does that. She describes a moment in each show when no arms remain crossed and the audience has become loose and relaxed—disarmed.

At the meet and greets that follow her shows, Anita hears a similar story, again and again: *I didn't want to come here tonight, but my sister/best friend/husband made me.* Maybe a spouse recently passed away. Or a child. Maybe a battle with disease or depression has left wounds that gape too wide to imagine they could ever be filled. Against their will they come—to make someone else happy—and sit in their so-numb-it's-become-comfortable shell and listen until a tiny crack appears. And then it happens: they laugh. Probably guiltily at first—you can be so entrenched in sorrow that it feels disloyal to shake it loose—but then they allow their spirit to infuse with joy and laugh deep and long. It's in that moment that they know: *I will make it. I will be okay.*

After church I sit down to lunch with two women who've been my friends for over twenty years. I believed that friendships like these could weather any storm, but recent months cast long shadows and honestly, I just want to walk in the sunshine again. Conversation begins gingerly—we've learned to tiptoe, to avoid the cracks—until we find that place only accessible through years of shared experiences and the deepest of friendships. It feels like home.

We talk of life goals that are out of our reach and body changes that are out of our control, and our conversation gets a little naughty, in the oh-so-mild version of the word that might be expected of forty- and fifty-something ladies sitting at a table in the church fellowship hall. We grin wide and our laughter rings so loud, so true, it attracts attention. People smile and nod at us because they know what I've only just realized. *We're going to make it. We're going to be okay.*

God used this season while I worked on this book about friendship to show me how important friendship is in my life and how hard I will fight to keep it alive. I've disagreed with friends on deep issues, and even when no one switched sides we held fast to each other and proved our relationships weren't superficial. I've leaned on mostly online but occasionally real-life friends. Don't let anyone tell you that a friendship that begins online must lack a foundation. Treasure friendship in whatever form it takes.

Although I envy those with a gift for digging deeper and encouraging others to open up more than they would otherwise, it's not my natural tendency. I'm a peacemaker by nature. I avoid ruffling feathers. Combine that with a hyperawareness of personal boundaries and privacy, and I can keep people at a distance. But sometimes you have to gently probe to take a relationship beyond shallow waters. I don't want to be afraid to ask hard questions, to bear burdens, to encourage truth and honesty.

Some relationships are ready-made: your kids play for the same team, you're in the same book club, or you take your little ones to the same playgroup. Others require work, when distance and schedules separate rather than connect. Some friendships must be intentionally pursued. Four of our kids ran cross-country recently, a sport that transitioned us from the heat of summer to the cooler days of early fall. My kids made new friends and so did I. Cross-country moms see each other at their worst: 8:00 a.m. practices in sweats and no makeup, unwashed hair, and that funky smell of post-workout sweat. It creates fertile ground for honest friendships. These women experienced me at my grungiest.

At the end-of-season party, the moms' conversations reflected relationships grown more than skin-deep: a child's lingering illness, plans to recertify and pursue professions that were put on hold during the early parenting years, my new work in book publishing. More than one eye brimmed with tears as we said goodbye.

And then we decided we didn't have to. The season had ended, but why must our friendships? We hastily scheduled a moms' night out at a new Mexican restaurant, because

17

less-than-concrete plans often amount to nothing more than good intentions. Next time we plan to go bowling.

You may be in a season where friendships seem scarce. Maybe you're new to your area, tangled in toddlers, or working long hours outside the home. Maybe you're self-sufficient and tend to keep to yourself. Even the most independent—and certainly the most isolated—among us need friends. We worship a relational God Who calls us to serve one another. He endows us with gifts—encouragement, hospitality, giving, wisdom—which can be fully expressed within the bounds of friendship.

While building long-term friendships is always a goal, I think sometimes God places people in our paths for a few moments, an hour, a day. Maybe it's the new mom sitting next to you in the pediatrician's office or the older woman in front of you in the checkout line or the twenty-something beside you in the conference hall. Conversations evolve in which words ring so true, so necessary, that a chance meeting feels anything but accidental. I feel like God grants us micro friendships—together for a reason in a season—when we connect briefly but meaningfully.

In mid-December a woman waved me to her table in a crowded mall food court when she saw I couldn't find a place to sit. I enjoyed forty-five minutes of conversation with her and her friend. We talked about motherhood, education, how our families celebrate Christmas. I heard words that I needed to hear and shared a lovely lunch with two ladies I'll probably never meet again. God moved in the middle, aware that I needed connection more than solitude. Don't miss small opportunities to speak a friendly word or provide a listening ear.

I believe the stories in this book will encourage you in your friendships because *that's what they've done for me.* I've arranged them into nine categories: "Building Community," "It Takes a Friend to Be a Friend," "Pursuing Friendship," "Hospitality," "Friendship on Purpose," "What I Learned about Friendship from My Family," "Vulnerability," "Making a Difference," and "Old Friends." I hope you find your own stories reflected in the words on these pages. I pray they spur you to step outside your comfort zone in the pursuit of friendship; to do what it takes to heal past wounds; to open the doors of your home and your heart; to love on the people around you; and to bask in the joy, the beauty, the *gift* of friendship.

Share this book with a friend and tell her how much she means to you: "Read this story. It's how I feel about us!"

Often it's the little things that keep us connected. It might be as simple as a timely text, a card in the mail, a phone call while running errands. Be the one to initiate a girls' night out. Just don't fail to express the simple but powerful message: I'm thinking of you. "A man that hath friends must shew himself friendly" (Prov. 18:24).

We need our people. We need friends standing in our corner, cheering us on, believing in us. We need listening ears, sharers of inside jokes, keepers of secrets. We need those who laugh when we laugh, cry when we cry, and then pass the chips and salsa. We need someone to look us in the eye and say, "You're my favorite."

And that's what it's all about. That's *the gift of friendship.*

Blessings,
Dawn

building
community

It is in the shelter of each other that the people live.

Irish Proverb

when friendship is more than favors

becky keife

I leaned against my kitchen sink—the one stacked with enough dirty dishes to hide the mysterious brown spots that needed to be scrubbed off—and took another deep breath.

It had been a long week. A long couple of months, really.

I felt so behind on ordinary life and I only half cared because the big, hard stuff that people I loved were going through made my crusty sink and loads of wrinkled laundry seem meaningless.

My mind spun with details of trying to arrange schedules and scrounge up childcare during my husband's busiest work season so I could go out of town to attend my friend's memorial service. My thirty-two-year-old, mother-of-two-little-ones, radiant friend who had lost her battle with cancer.

I desperately wanted to make the seven-hour road trip to gather with loved ones and celebrate her beautiful life. There were still so many pieces up in the air, but at least I had Desiree committed to caring for my youngest son. I glanced back at the dishes and picked up my phone instead. It was hard to think through the heart-swirling emotions and mind-whirling list of to-dos. But I managed to pluck out a text to Des with a few more details about my departure and drop-off plans, and rambled a list of thanks for all the other ways she had recently helped me.

I finished the text with this heart confession:

"I feel like I've been a really needy friend lately and you are always there to help so willingly. Thank you. I appreciate you beyond words and hope that at some point I can return all the favors."

Within a moment I heard the familiar bing-bong of a new message.

She wrote back: "Don't be silly! Friendship is way more than favors. It's life together! I love you dearly."

I read her words. Then read them again. Slowly allowing each one to mark my heart like the fresh tears staining my cheeks.

My dear friend was so right. Friendship is way more than favors.

In fact, that's something I would have said had our roles been reversed. It's my joy to help my friends! I'm thankful when I'm able to meet a tangible need for someone I care for or come alongside a friend to understand their hurts or celebrate their triumphs.

But as the one who had to do the help-asking, as the one whose tears flowed frequently, whose practical and emotional needs had been many, I'd fallen into a guilt trap of thinking that *I* was too much. Of believing that my friends were keeping a tally of helps poured out, a record of favors given and favors owed.

I felt like as soon as life calmed down and I got my act together, I would need to start paying back all the good deeds done for me to even the score.

But the truth is, friends, there is no score-keeping when doing life together.

What is there, then? There is community-building by bearing each other's burdens, and sometimes that means being willing to let yourself be the one carried.

Several days later I pulled into Desiree's driveway and unloaded my two-year-old and his backpack full of overnight gear. We walked up the terra-cotta path, and he stood on tippy toes to reach the doorbell. When Des opened the door, my son happily joined the beautiful chaos of a home full of small children and lots of love.

And I hugged my sweet friend, comforted by the assurance that she was happy to be doing life together, which today meant serving me by loving my son.

No one is useless in this world who lightens the burdens of another.

Charles Dickens, *Doctor Marigold*

the patchwork of humanity

sarah forgrave

y mom used to make quilts when I was little.[1] I suppose it's a natural part of living in Amish country. She would bundle me up and we'd go to the fabric store, where she would pore over bolts of cloth until she found just the right mix. Solids, patterns, florals—they all played a key role.

She would return home and set to work cutting out scraps of cloth then sewing them into squares. When all the squares were ready, she'd pull out the massive quilt frame that took up half our living room and piece all the squares together. Several weeks later we'd have a new bedspread, a quilt with an intricate pattern made unique by the placement of its individual squares.

I recently came across a different kind of quilt—a quilt made up of several different pieces of fabric, all equally

---

1. Sarah Forgrave, "The Patchwork of Humanity," originally published in *Ungrind*, July 25, 2013, http://ungrind.org/2013/the-patchwork-of-humanity/.

beautiful and valuable in their contribution to the bigger picture.

I call it the patchwork of humanity.

It happened at the moms' group at my church. I arrived for the first meeting of the year, signed in, and grabbed a badge with my name preprinted on it. Fifteen minutes later I learned that my name badge had a code. The badges were split into three colors, and my color represented which small group I would join for the year.

As we all dispersed into our separate groups, I glanced at the women around me and wondered what the year might hold. I hadn't met many of them before, and I questioned what would happen if I didn't mesh with the people around me.

The leader welcomed us and shared her excitement about the coming year. Then she explained her vision for the group. Specifically, she wanted us to become a support system for each other, going beyond prayer requests that spanned ailing grandparents and travel safety and moving toward a community that was open and honest about our struggles at home.

I sat there quietly listening as doubts assailed me. Surely openness and honesty couldn't be forced. What if these people didn't want to dive beyond the surface? What then?

In five short minutes, my doubts were squelched.

I started the introductions and shared about my family, my work, and my passion for writing. The next girl shared about her husband's call to the ministry but expressed uncertainty at the waiting game in which they found themselves. A couple more introductions later, things got more intense.

A woman I'd never met before opened up about the problems she faced at home—a major disagreement with her husband that had her surviving on three hours of sleep most days. Her emotions were raw, and as she poured out her heart the group became silent. My throat grew thick as I thought about her struggle and put myself in her skin.

Then the next woman spoke. I don't remember if she officially introduced herself or not. All I remember is that one of the first things she said was that she and her husband were going through a divorce. She had a young son at home and talked about her concerns for him. Her voice broke, and the thickness in my throat exploded to my eyes. I felt the sting of her pain, my heart stretching out of my chest and yearning to cradle that small child in my arms.

Fifteen years ago, my parents divorced.

I grabbed a tissue from my purse and offered it to her. In that brief moment when we both touched the same piece of paper, I realized that God had shattered my preconceptions. He had linked me to these women I'd never met in a powerful way, a way that went beyond human logic and bias.

On the drive home, one image kept dominating my thoughts. A quilt. A comforter like my mom used to make, blending solids, patterns, and florals.

Some of the fabrics were colorful and vibrant, while others faded into the background or had frayed around the edges. The quilt maker took those frayed pieces and stitched them next to a sturdy piece. As each scrap of cloth connected with another, the weak ones became stronger, until the squares were stitched together to form a quilt. A quilt with no evidence of frayed edges. A quilt as beautiful as its most vibrant pattern.

The image took prominence in my brain, and I realized that this was what God has called me to. He wants me to step out and share my deepest hurts and fears with a trusted group, to let others come alongside me and trim off my frayed edges. Or in those moments when I'm sturdy, He stitches me next to someone else to hold them together.

I love how *The Message* paraphrases 1 Thessalonians 5:11:

> So speak encouraging words to one another. Build up hope so you'll all be together in this, no one left out, no one left behind.

As an introvert, I would find it so easy to stay hidden away in the back of the linen closet, to tackle life alone, to assume that no one else wants to know about all my problems. But to follow through on that would mean missing out on the hope God designed for His church. He doesn't want to see anyone left out or left behind.

When I step out of my box, I subject myself to potential pain, the prick of the quilter's needle. Life is messy. Not everyone lives a rosy existence. And often the struggles of others remind us of our own struggles, just like the divorced mother's pain resurrected my own buried pain that day. The heaviness that used to haunt me landed on my shoulders all over again in that one moment.

But by simply being there, I allowed God to patch me together with other women whose lives were frayed just like mine. Some of us had to endure a lot more trimming than others, and some of us had smaller scraps to contribute. Whether solids or patterns, we all melded together in a beautiful work of art. And in that moment, I gained new hope because I joined God's greater masterpiece.

The patchwork of humanity.

Christ, Who said to the disciples, "Ye have not chosen me, but I have chosen you," can truly say to every group of Christian friends, "Ye have not chosen one another but I have chosen you for one another." The friendship is not a reward for our discriminating and good taste in finding one another out. It is the instrument by which God reveals to each of us the beauties of others.

C. S. Lewis, *The Four Loves*

building community in an unexpected place
dawn camp

"Welcome to Moe's!" shout the employees in unison from behind the counter as hungry customers enter on kids' night. On a typical weeknight we join six or more families for food, fun, and fellowship in this restaurant where we've nurtured community in an unexpected place.

It began, simply enough, as an occasional night out. With time, however, it has become an almost indispensable part of our family routine: a place to gather once a week with friends to talk sports, current events, and religion; to discuss our kids' classes; to celebrate birthdays.

We love the food—and obviously the moms enjoy a night out of the kitchen—but it's the fellowship that brings us back week after week. The kids play with decks of cards, climb the tree beside the door, or even play Frisbee or football outside when the weather is warm. The employees make us feel welcome and appreciated even though we're a large, sometimes noisy crowd that tends to stay until closing time (or beyond). These evenings benefit us all, but I think the men profit the most. My husband spends his days at work and his weekends at home and church. Although the kids and I have day-to-day friends—families we spend time with at homeschool classes and events—my husband is rarely a part of it.

Moe's nights bring the husbands together. They enjoy crowding around a table for guy talk as much as the women and kids enjoy their time. Sometimes we just stop and listen to them, savoring the sounds of male camaraderie as they strengthen friendships.

Life is busy. If you don't make time to get together, once-solid friendships can fall victim to neglect. But Wednesday nights are easy, these meet-in-the-middle meals with no cooking or cleaning required. Our weekly evenings at Moe's have become an important family tradition. I savor this community we've grown in an unexpected place.

If more of us valued food and cheer and song above hoarded gold,
it would be a merrier world.

J. R. R. Tolkien, *The Hobbit*

in which i tell the truth about women and community

alia joy hagenbach

J fingered the insert in the church bulletin with disdain. *Seriously? A teddy bear tea party?* I was twenty years old! *Why was women's ministry so antiquated?*

The men's ministry was heading off to shoot clay pigeons for their gathering, and we had to scrounge up teddy bears and doilies and nibble on soggy triangles of cucumber and Miracle Whip smooshed into crustless Wonderbread?

I envisioned the small church drenched in floral tablecloths and copious amounts of pink. I pictured a leader with coiffed hair, a below-the-knee-length skirt, and lipstick in a bright berry hue who would give a cursory overview of Proverbs 31, the Book of Ruth or Esther, and women's roles as homemakers and baby ovens.

Needless to say, I didn't go. In fact, community with women had been conspicuously absent in my life for years. I had mountains of hurt that stemmed from female gatherings as a girl and as a woman.

Now, a teddy bear tea party still isn't my cup of tea, no pun intended, but I have come to realize that in my judgments of other women I've done a great disservice to the fabric of community.

After fourteen years, I've realized that there are so many ways God made women and that we are always stronger together than alone.

There is something to be said for a woman who can knit doilies or crochet or make cowls that fasten loosely around your neck and feel like a hug from a friend.

There is something magnificent in a woman who goes out to run when it's seven degrees outside and the air chills her lungs and short puffs of cottony white trail her as her legs pump.

There is something glorious about a bleary-eyed woman who tucks her nursing baby against her and gives her life away in the wee hours of morning.

There is something brilliant in a woman whose brows knit together in concentration when she tackles problems at work, considers how to best fix the hack job her three-year-old did to her hair when no one was looking, or writes down her grocery list.

There is something majestic about the older woman who has served until her weathered hands grip the pages of her battleworn Bible with spidery veins snaking across parchment skin.

There is something pristine about the fresh-faced college girl who reaches out for wisdom and finds it not only in the peers who walk with her but in the grandmother who walked before her.

There is something to be said for women in all their unique glory and splendor, and there is something so very beautiful about the gift and sisterhood of friends.

We are the world changers, ladies. We carry communities and speak into each other's lives. We raise babies into men and women. We teach souls and feed minds. We nourish each other with words of encouragement. We mourn and rejoice

and give our lives away in casseroles and hugs, coffee dates
and carpools.

We are the laborers birthing new life as we speak the gospel
into emptiness and heal each other.

We do the work of God's heart as we tend to each other
and love one another and lean hard into Christ's side.

Friendship is unnecessary, like philosophy, like art . . . .
It has no survival value; rather it is one of those things
which give value to survival.

C. S. Lewis, The Four Loves

fans in the stands

laura parker

J am relearning community in new ways here in Colorado. I'm intersecting with people whom I remember were around when I had my babies and when we didn't have a car. I'm gathering around a fire pit with coffee and wine with friends who know our story, even the ugly parts of it. And I'm emergency texting prayer requests and "What do you want from Starbucks?" on those days when human interaction beats screen time a million to one. I've tasted holy vulnerability under a mountain and over a sushi lunch on a normal Tuesday, talked about things that really matter while circuit training in a gym, and listened to a first reading of a screenplay written by friends that I'm sure I'll be watching in theaters before too long.

And I've been reminded of the goodness of having someone else's back, of being in someone else's corner. And I'm tasting the transformative power of knowing that the same goes for me too. Because whether we like to admit it or not: We. Need. People. We need fans in our stands, those who believe we can rise above whatever we've done or whatever was done to us—or maybe both.

And we can wait around for community to happen to us and then complain when it might not, or we can pursue it and fight for it like our lives depend on it.

Because they do.

There is nothing I would not do for those who are really my friends. I have no notion of loving people by halves, it is not my nature.

Jane Austen, *Northanger Abbey*

unscheduled time with friends—for the sake of our sanity

francie winslow

When was the last day you enjoyed unscheduled time catching up with an old friend or getting to know someone new?

Most parts of my average suburban life feel planned, scheduled, and busy. Dare I linger longer than usual after church? Or hang out by the mailbox just to chat with the elderly lady next door? Or listen to a hurting mom at the playground when I really need to be grocery shopping? *I can't,* I usually think to myself. *I just don't have the time.*

Part of this "I just can't" feeling is directly related to the ages of my young kids. Some days they feel like ticking time bombs. If we don't keep moving with the next thing—our scheduled lunch, nap, park time, or whatever may be the next part of our day—they just might explode.

Another reason for my "I just can't" feeling is the idea that I must be doing something important or productive in order for my days to be valuable. I can be so busy being productive that I forget to make room for the most important thing of all. Relationships.

Until recently, that is.

A few weeks ago, I hosted a MOPS (Mothers of Preschoolers) playdate at my house with the ladies who have been at my table all year. It was *planned* to be from ten to noon. Just as planned as all of our other meetings.

With nothing truly pressing to do, however, two friends from the group stayed several hours after the playdate officially ended. It was an unplanned, spontaneous, and relationally deepening time.

At first, to be honest, I was a little uncomfortable. I thought, *Wait—we need to end this. It's nap time! We have a schedule and we try really hard to follow it every day . . . for the sake of all our sanity!*

But much to my surprise, I looked around and noticed that all of our kids were content without their regularly planned naps. We moms were happy holding our glasses of tea and letting go of our to-do lists for the day.

I don't recommend throwing out your schedule every day, but maybe this kind of unscheduled hang-out time every now and then is actually more helpful for our sanity than we realize.

Spending time deepening our relationships is an essential part of our well-being in this world of high-tech, high-speed, and highly connected social (but not deeply relational) media. These days we are always connected—but rarely known. And isn't being known what we really crave?

That summer afternoon we simply enjoyed time together. We sat in the warm sun, watched our kids play, and heard each other's stories.

We relished one another.

And sure enough, I got to know those two ladies more in that one unplanned afternoon than I did through a whole year of planned meetings.

Long gone are the days when people just stop by to say hi. Or to sit in rocking chairs on the front porch and catch up on the family comings and goings. I actually never really knew those times, just heard tell of them. And even though I never really lived them, I miss them.

I miss being with people just to be with them. I was filled up and refreshed by spontaneous quality time with new friends that afternoon, and I'd like more of that in my life.

Don't get me wrong. Schedules are key. I live a very focused life. And having a schedule actually brings freedom to do more of what is important every day.

But from now on, I want to arrange my schedule so that it frees me up for more unscheduled relationship-building time. I want to intentionally prioritize a certain level of margin that creates room for authentic relationships to bloom and friendships to deepen.

Because life is just better when we have the space to know and be known by friends.

I count myself in nothing else so happy as in a soul remembering my good friends.

William Shakespeare, *Richard II*   41

it takes a friend to be a friend

He that is thy friend indeed,
He will help thee in thy need:
If thou sorrow, he will weep;
If thou wake, he cannot sleep:
Thus of every grief in heart
He with thee doth bear a part.
These are certain signs to know
Faithful friend from flattering foe.

Richard Barnfield, "An Ode"

the one thing every good friend does

kristen strong

We sit in the chilled fall air at a downtown cafe, coats on and twin cupcakes on the table between us. She talks about big things going on in her life, golden-edged things welcomed after a season of hard nos. She is teary and grateful. I listen enthusiastically because part of me comes alive when I get to hear other people share their good news and realized dreams.

I imagine God sitting there with us, enjoying His daughters enjoying community.

After we lick the last traces of cupcake frosting from our fingers, she apologizes for monopolizing the conversation. I wave my hand and tell her she didn't monopolize it one bit. She *shined* in the conversation, for the love. And I am happy to give her the space to do so because it means she trusts me enough to let me cup a bit of her heart in my hands.

I could make a too-long list of all the times I haven't had gracious intentions toward friends. Sometimes I care more about what I want to say than what I want to hear. If the scales tip because I do this too much, then I'm not being the best kind of friend.

Because the truth is this: if you want to be a friend to someone, you must reconcile the fact that you don't always get to have your say. You have to care more about listening than talking.

Of course, a hallmark of great friendship is when both women share in equal parts. But sometimes—in a single conversation or over a season—we place our own words on an altar as we listen with abandon.

Is this hard to do? Sometimes. Is it worth the effort? Always.

If community wasn't important, Jesus wouldn't have chosen to get His sandals dusty in the middle of it. But He did, and He was the best kind of listener while doing so. Humility is the heartbeat of all encouragement, and it takes humility to sit with hands and heart open and lips closed. It takes security to know that listening to a friend share her victories and blessings doesn't diminish our own choices and abilities. It takes compassion to know that listening to her share her struggles and losses doesn't elevate our status in the imaginary Woman Who Most Has Her Act Together challenge. It takes a true sister to cheer on another sister in ways that make both women come alive.

It takes a friend, a good friend.

When we give cheerfully and accept gratefully, everyone is blessed.

Maya Angelou (attributed)

we found them

sophie hudson

For the last couple of weeks my son Alex and I have been playing a silly game. He'll walk up to me and say, "What's your name?"

And I'll say something silly like "Snickerbottoms" or "Picklelemons" or "McTuttlenuts."

And then he'll feign surprise and say, "My name is Snickerbottoms too! I found you! We must be family!" and then he throws his arms around me and laughs hysterically and wants to play the game all over again.

He loves it. I do too.

Last year—The Two-Oh-Oh-Eight—was wonderful and exciting and challenging and hard. It was overwhelming at times. There were some difficult patches for sure, and I'm being as vague as possible, you see, because let's keep it light, people. Let's keep it light and then let's laugh about something—this is how I operate.

So, in short: while there were definitely some bright spots, more often than not in 2008 it seemed like I was forever standing before God and just flat-out wrestling with all my stinkin' sin and mistakes and selfishness and failures and stubbornness. And fear. Oh my word, the fear. And worry. And so on and so forth.

But.

In the midst of all that.

God did the coolest thing.

I have long contended that I have the sweetest friends and family in the whole wide world, and if you don't believe me then you should meet them—and then you'd see and then you'd probably want to be friends with them too, and that

is understandable, really, because they are all quite fabulous. Most of those sweet friends have been in my life since high school or college, and I kid you not that one of the great delights of my life is laughing with them about everything and nothing. Those girls know my faults like nobody's business (I'm prideful, I don't like to talk about my problems or my weaknesses, I'm moody, and the list goes on and on) and love me anyway. And I love them to pieces.

So in terms of longtime friends, I've been beyond blessed. But truth be told, I struggle sometimes when new people come along because I feel like I'm not serious enough or smart enough or holy enough or laid-back enough or disciplined enough or whatever, not to mention that I'm irreverent and sarcastic (I'm going to start calling it "sar*tastic*," by the way) and loud and waist-deep in the process of working out my junk and figuring out what it means to live a fully surrendered life. (Oh, sweet mercy, I feel that I've hit my introspective limit for 2009 already and please, can we just talk about bacon?)

Anyway, the bottom line is this: I can get pretty comfortable with (relative) isolation if I'm not careful. I can start to *like* isolation if I'm not careful. The fact that I don't blog about all the "issues" in my life and my family's life doesn't make them go away, and if for some reason you think I don't have "issues," then permit me to give you this piece of advice: oh please, don't kid yourself.

But in 2008, despite all the life junk, God just blessed our socks off through people. Old friends. New friends who were "hit it off" people to such a degree that it almost gave me whiplash. Their names aren't "Snickerbottoms" or "Picklelemons" or "McTuttlenuts," but almost every single time I talk to them I want to throw my arms around them and hug them to pieces and scream, "We found you! We must be family!"

So while it's tempting for me to look back on last year and think mostly about the hard things, what I want to remember about last year are the *best* things. Because I'll tell you this right now, and you can cross-stitch it and frame it and hang it in your living room in the dead-dog center of your wall if you'd like: it's a whole lot easier to walk through your "issues" when there are people in your life whom you love and trust—and when they love and trust you right back. Whether they're family, old friends, or new friends, I don't want to do life without them.

A man that hath friends must shew himself friendly: and there is a friend that sticketh closer than a brother.

Proverbs 18:24

on friendship

ruth chou simons

It's not every day The Preacher and I sit down to a meal with another couple who, like us, have founded a school that they now head. Like us, they are classical, Christian, and university model. Our new friends sought to know us better over a fire-roasted artichoke at The Cheesecake Factory. The Preacher and I found ourselves recounting the past year or so of our lives. As we shared, a theme emerged: one of sickness, relational wounds, the loss of close friends and family as they moved away, and deep concern and counsel within ministry. Our bird's-eye view revealed what a difficult year we'd had— each month highlighted with joys, yes, but distinctly marked by the testing of our faith and burdened hearts. Of the many lessons learned about gratitude, contentment, forgiveness, and faith this last year, the greatest has been the overarching picture of delighting in Christ alone.

Not to serve Him mechanically or routinely but to worship and adore Him gratefully.

Not to view Him as distant and aloof but to recognize the nearness of Him who carries our greatest burdens.

Not to withdraw from our Maker when we are afraid but to run to Him in desperation.

Not to consider ourselves merely subjects but rather intimate friends of the King.

To have friendship with God is to enjoy Him, to be intimate with Him, to be invited into the Oneness of the Trinity. What a marvel it is that God allows us to mirror that love and friendship within the body of Christ. That we can know true friendship with others. Our Latin students learned to recite this from Cicero's *De Amicitia* this past year:

Pauci viri veros amicos habent, et pauci sunt digni. Amicitia vera est praeclara, et omnia praeclara sunt rara. Multi viri stulti de pecunia semper cogitant, pauci de amicis; sed errant: possumus valere sine multa pecunia, sed sine amicitia non valemus et vita est nihil.

It translates:

Few men have true friends, and few are worthy. True friendship is splendid, and all things precious are rare. Many foolish men always think about money, few about friends; but they err: we can be well without much money, but without friendship we are not well and life is nothing.

There's no greater time than times of trials to bring to light the value of true friendships, and the true nature of the friendships you value. Indeed, few have true friends, and true friends are few and far between.

A man of many companions may come to ruin, but there is a friend who sticks closer than a brother.

Proverbs 18:24 ESV

Take heart, friend. If today finds you aching in body or in heart, our Father is near; He is a true friend. You need no one but Him, yet our God is good and gives us more than what we need. He also gives us what we desire and provides true friendships. You have need of only a few . . . *invest wisely.*

Henceforth I call you not servants; for the servant knoweth not what his lord doeth: but I have called you friends; for all things that I have heard of my Father I have made known unto you.

John 15:15

on the kind of friend i want my daughter to have

anna rendell

*L*ast week some friends of mine were talking about their first- and second-grade daughters, specifically the nitty-gritty of the girls' friendships. They said their girls will tell them that one day they're best friends with so-and-so, but the next day the friendship is over. Their girls said the conversations go like this:

> You sat by her during story time. We're not friends anymore.
>
> You smiled at her in the hallway. We're not friends anymore.
>
> You're playing flute instead of clarinet? We're not friends anymore.

One said when her granddaughter was young, she and a friend made a "we're not eating tuna fish" pact. One day the granddaughter brought a tuna fish sandwich to lunch and ate it, so her friend said their friendship was over. Because of tuna fish.

I've heard dozens of these stories over the years. Parents of kids in my youth group, hoping church would be a safe place. Campers, offering their personal stories within the safety of the bunk beds. Young staff, learning how to transition high school relationships to college. Articles in magazines. Moms in online parenting groups. This is a very real epidemic that we can dismiss as "kids being kids," or worse, as "girls being girls." But is this how we want to define our girls? Do we want our little girls learning to threaten with their friendship?

This is so, so not finger-pointing at anyone except myself. These are all things I've done to my friends:

Get a text that you disagree with? Don't respond. Ignore her.

She parents her kids differently than you? Don't set up another playtime. Pull away.

Jealous of the promotion or opportunity she got? Don't congratulate. Mutter to yourself how it should've been yours.

She misspoke or made a mistake? Don't tell her. Instead, tell another friend about your hurt feelings.

There is power in friendship. If it didn't matter, threatening to end it wouldn't be our knee-jerk reaction. We know what will sting, we know the intricate ways we can intentionally hurt another, and we know how to craft a phrase so it drips with veiled jabs. There is power in our presence and in our friendship, and we can use both of them either to build up or to punish.

I'm tired. I'm tired of watching dramas unfold in green text bubbles. I'm tired of the unfriending, the unfollowing, the blocking. I'm tired of hurting for my daughter's heart that's not even been scarred yet. I'm tired of staying up into the wee hours of the night rephrasing words already spoken, replaying scenes already played, reminding myself of relationships lost.

My heart is tired of seeing women hurt one another. Search "how to be a good friend" and you'll see thousands of options. Search "how to stop a bully" and you'll get just as many.

We talk about a tribe, about a village, about being family. But the words are naught but clanging cymbals without love-based action.

I don't want to hear stories like the ones above from my daughter. Of course heartbreak happens. Of course you can't be friends with everyone. But if I want my daughter to know how to be a good friend, I need to be the one to show her. I need to treat my friends with respect and with kindness, giving them the benefit of the doubt. I need to rise above my old and deep-set habit of passive-aggressive polite. I need to model friendship on purpose.

It starts with us, moms. It starts with a deep breath. It starts with responding when we don't want to. It starts with praying over our words before pressing "send." It starts with simple honesty when it would be easier to stay silent. It starts with asking the hard questions and being willing to answer them ourselves. It starts in our kitchens, in our living rooms, on our phones, and with our coffeepots. It starts in our own lives and it starts in our own hearts.

I'm putting out a call to be brave. To embrace the sweetness and the depth of real friendship. To hold ourselves to a higher standard than silence. To become the kind of friend we pray our daughters have. This kind of friendship isn't easy. It's hard and messy and can come with real heartache. But it can also come with richness and love and someone to really do life with too, and it is so worth it.

We don't learn to love each other well in the easy moments. Anyone is good company at a cocktail party. But love is born when we misunderstand one another and make it right, when we cry in the kitchen, when we show up uninvited with magazines and granola bars, in an effort to say, I love you.

Shauna Niequist, *Bread & Wine*

behind the door

lesli richards

*H*er sparkling blue eyes and her wide smile made her seem like an instant friend. Have you ever felt that way about someone you've just met? The room was filled with a hundred women at that MOPS group, but she was the one who linked arms with me and took me to her table and into her tribe. She was so open and happy, and so irreverently funny. I laughed more that day than I had in a long time. It had been a long year of growing up . . . adding a new baby and losing my beloved grandmother and father-in-law. I felt like I was still trying to master adult life . . . parenting, marriage, and especially housekeeping. While I loved my new little family, many days I felt like I was just treading water, trying to keep my head above all my new duties and roles. I swallowed a lot of water in those days!

You see, I grew up in a home with a single working mother in the seventies. She was a free spirit and didn't take to routines, so I grew up without an internal schedule of the way things run in a house. We didn't have regular meals. When we were hungry, we would slide out the wooden breadboard from the counter and pull out pickles, olives, salami, and whatever else we could find, and we'd stand in the kitchen and eat and chat. We cleaned at Christmas, I think. And if my mom had a date. So, predictably, when I went off to college my roommates had to have a little sit-down with me about vacuuming and dusting. I didn't mind cleaning, I just didn't know *when* to clean. When I became a Christian, I really embraced the idea of being a Proverbs 31 wife, and figured that God and I would eventually flesh that out together.

So when I settled into married life I checked out books on housekeeping and made myself charts for chores. But always, the perfectly kept home eluded me. I loved the life of the mind, and being a new believer was giving me lots to think about. I loved reading thoughtful books by old dead guys and having long phone conversations about them with friends. I loved art and sewing projects, and cooking complicated recipes that used every bowl in the house. Adding two babies compounded the disorder. My sweet neatnik husband would come home, open the door, and survey the damage before cheerfully helping clean up after our day of adventures. Poor man. It was bad. Seriously bad. As a matter of fact, I once called the police on myself because I unlocked the front door of our apartment to find all of the drawers open and ransacked. As I dialed 911 and waited, I realized I'd made the mess myself while looking for my keys. That is pretty humbling. I started to feel ashamed and defeated. I stopped inviting people over. My natural hospitality withered. I would visit other people's beautifully kept homes and feel so much self-loathing. Eventually I stopped inviting people over, and the doorbell was a dreaded sound. Why in the world was it so hard for me?

So you can see why, that day at a MOPS meeting, her smiling face was a balm to my soul. After I left, I kept thinking about her. I worked up enough courage to call her and asked her and her children to spend the day at the aquarium with my children and me. That call turned into an hour-long side-splitting conversation, and I hung up looking forward to our day out in the big city. In the morning, I made sure that we were all ready and standing on the porch when she arrived . . . I didn't want my new cool friend to see that I hadn't done the breakfast dishes or that there was a pile of laundry on the couch. We readjusted five car seats and climbed in the car. She turned the key. Click. No engine sound. I ran into the house and got the cordless phone and called AAA to come jump her car. I didn't invite her in or suggest we let the children out of the car to play. I just prayed that the tow truck would miraculously sprout wings like *Chitty Chitty Bang Bang* and get us on our way. Our babies fell asleep in the car. And we waited. And waited. And then I felt it. I was nursing a massive baby with a voracious appetite at the time, and my body apparently felt it was time to feed his sleeping self. Before the great flood could ruin my well-planned outfit . . . I ran into the house and got my breast pump and sat in her front seat in all my glory and pumped out a couple of bottles of milk.

I hope it isn't lost on you that I was more willing to show this woman my *naked breasts* than my house.

But eventually the tow truck came and rescued us, and off we went. We had a great day. Our kids were the same ages and were instantly thick as thieves. We talked and laughed all day as we explored the aquarium full of God's glorious unexpected creatures. It was a day brimming with joy—tow trucks, breast pumps, and all.

On our way home, my friend turned to me and said something amazing. She said, "You know, I've had so much fun with you, I just don't want this day to end. Call your husband and have him come over to my house, and we will all have dinner." I was thrilled to be invited, and my husband agreed. We pulled up in front of her house and she opened the door. I looked around in amazement. The sink was full of dishes. There was laundry on the couch. There were footie pajamas and school books on the floor. But spending time with me was more important to her than worrying about what I might think about her house. My eyes filled with tears. Together we folded laundry and did the dishes and made a meal for our husbands while our children played. That day was a holy blessing to me, one of the most sacred days of my life. She taught me to never again shut the door on fellowship because I'm ashamed of what's behind the door.

That day was only the beginning of our friendship. We grew up together in our young marriedness. We decided that it was more fun to clean together while our children played, so we just moved from one house to the other with our aprons and cleaning supplies. God knit our hearts together in so many ways in those years. I cried buckets when her husband was transferred and they moved to the Northwest. I will always love her madly, because she changed me. She didn't make me neater but she made me more loving and more open. She made me a better friend. You can thank her when I invite you in to step over my mess and into my real and authentic life.

We all have a mess somewhere, and we can use it as an excuse not to love people the way God wants us to love. But God wants us to live in open fellowship with each other. Not in competition or shame. Proverbs 17:17 tells us that "a friend loveth at all times," and I take that to mean at *all* times—not just when our house is ready for the *Southern Living* photography team.

They are funny, our ages and stages. I'd thought I'd slayed the home-keeping beast. I'd had a good routine going for years. My house has been home base for lots of laughter and impromptu dinner parties. But writing two books and having teenagers and a lot of littles has given me some setbacks in the past couple of years. My doorbell rings and I find myself apologizing again. Thankfully I'm no longer nursing, so the world is at least safe from that, but do me a favor. Stop by. Unannounced. Give me the opportunity to say yes to fellowship and openness. Scold me if I apologize. Help me fold my laundry. Love me where I'm at. Because life is a struggle and it's hard for all of us at one point or another—and that comes as no surprise to God. He knows what's behind the door and He loves you anyway.

Friendship is born at that moment when one man says to another: "What! You too?"

C. S. Lewis, *The Four Loves*

how do you find good friends?

crystal paine

If you've read my book *Say Goodbye to Survival Mode*, you know that I struggled with friendships for the first twenty-eight or so years of my life. A lot of this had to do with my insecure, people-pleasing personality. I had been hurt deeply by people close to me in the past, so I had spent years of my life too scared to open up or be authentic for fear of getting hurt again.

But finally I was so tired of living life feeling so lonely that I knew something needed to change. And that something was me.

I had to stop trying to please people, stop staying closed up and closed off to avoid getting hurt, and start reaching out, being authentic, and being 100 percent me.

As a result of this shift in my thinking and change in my heart, I've developed some incredibly deep and authentic relationships that have been such an immense blessing to me!

And I've also learned a lot about what great friendships are made up of. Here are four components I believe are key to any strong relationship.

1. Honesty

If you want authentic relationships, you first have to be willing to be authentic yourself. You have to stop hiding behind a fake, people-pleasing persona and start being genuinely you.

Put down the plastic smiles, don't keep people at arm's length, and start letting people see you for exactly who you are—messes, struggles, and all. True friends don't want you to be perfect and all put-together.

> **Tip:** If someone doesn't love you for who you are but instead wants you to be who they want you to be, that's a good sign they aren't a true friend.

2. Commitment

True friendship requires commitment. It means that you will believe the best, you will speak the truth when it's needed, and you won't gossip or slander.

It means you are *for* the other person. You want them to succeed. You celebrate them. You appreciate them. You build them up when you speak to them face-to-face and when you talk about them to others.

> **Tip:** If someone just wants to be your friend for what you can do for them—not because they love you for who you are—they aren't a true friend.

3. Effort

A good friendship requires effort. It doesn't just happen. It means that both parties make sacrifices for each other.

Want to have great friends? *Start by being the friend to others that you wish you had yourself.* It means picking up the phone, taking time to text or email, and making time to get together for coffee.

Deep relationships take time and investment. They rarely happen overnight. Instead, they are the result of much cultivation, time, and effort.

> **Tip:** If you have reached out to someone multiple times and they are always too busy to spend time with you, that's probably a good indication it's time to move on to investing in another relationship.

4. Forgiveness

Close friendships will result in misunderstanding and hurt, at times. No one is always going to do everything right all the time. And the closer you are to someone, the more possibility there is for misunderstanding and hurt.

Some days, your friend might say something that frustrates or offends you. Some days, your friend might not respond how you wish she would. Some days, she's just plain going to bother or upset you. On those days, you have two choices: you can choose to forgive, or you can choose to be hurt and bitter.

Friendships that stand the test of time are ones where both parties choose to forgive when offenses and hurts come. It's not easy and it means having hard conversations and sometimes saying things that are difficult to say. But good communication, working through issues, and having a heart of forgiveness will only deepen a friendship.

Tip: If someone is easily offended and constantly being hurt or upset by you, there's a good chance they aren't a good friend.

How to Be a Good Friend

- **Take initiative.** Don't wait for others to make the first move. Ask your friend to meet for coffee, invite your friend over to hang out, or text her to tell her you're thinking of her. Reach out. Focus on blessing others and you'll often be richly blessed in return. If you are thinking of someone, let them know you're thinking of them. Often just taking the time to text or email someone to let them know they are on your heart that day can mean the world to them.

- **Have a listening ear.** People feel valued when you look them in the eye and genuinely listen to what they have to share. Give them your undivided attention. Don't think about what you're going to say next. Just listen wholeheartedly.

- **Ask good questions.** Be interested in others' lives. Learn about what they are excited about. Find out what their passions are. Ask about their goals and long-term dreams. Find out what they are struggling with. Ask how you can pray for them . . . and then actually follow through with praying for them! A question I sometimes

67

will ask is just, "How can I be a better friend to you?" The answers to that one might truly surprise you.

- **Find the good and praise it.** Constantly be looking for ways you can celebrate someone else. Take time to express appreciation. Don't just think it—stop and verbalize it.

- **Learn their love language.** How does your friend feel most loved? Is it by words of affirmation, a letter, gifts, acts of service? Knowing this can help you know how to love them best.

When we do the hard, intimate work of friendship, we bring a little more of the divine into daily life.

Shauna Niequist, Cold Tangerines

pursuing friendship

I look back now and realize that the gift of a true friend is that she sees you not the way you see yourself or the way others see you. A true friend sees you for who you are and who you can become.

Robin Jones Gunn, *Sister Chicks Say Ooh La La!*

friendship bread

a recipe worth sharing

liz curtis higgs

J'd never heard of friendship bread until my friend Pam
served it for lunch. I was hooked.

"Want some starter?" Pam handed over a plastic bag full
of glop and a recipe that had been photocopied dozens of
times. "It's easy to make."

The instructions were clear enough: "*Do not* use metal
spoon or bowl when mixing. *Do not* refrigerate." Then, this
ominous note: "It is *normal* for batter to thicken, bubble,
and ferment."

Ferment? Was I supposed to eat this? Too late. I'd already
eaten it.

"Leave it on the counter," Pam told me. "And *do not*
refrigerate."

"What about tomorrow?"

"Just squeeze it."

"You're kidding!"

"Read the recipe."

Days two, three, four, and five simply said, "Squeeze bag." This was my idea of baking. On day six I added flour, sugar, and milk but *did not* refrigerate. *Ick.* Three more days of squeezing, then I emptied everything into a big bowl. More flour, more sugar, more milk.

Here's where the starter is born. I divided the glop evenly into four portions, then poured three portions into plastic bags and set them aside to share with friends.

The time had finally come to bake my glop into bread. I poured my portion into a bowl—*not metal*—and stirred in oil, vanilla, eggs, a package of pudding, and baking power. That's not a typo. The recipe called for "1 teaspoon of baking *power*." Sure could use some of *that* at the Higgs house.

I dumped the mixture into two pans—sugared, not floured—and baked the loaves for an hour. Ta-da. Bread.

Except now I'd baked my starter and was left with nothing to squeeze for the next ten days. I'd have to wait until friends one, two, or three gave me a new bag of starter—actually, my own starter in another life. And who knows? The friendship bread I'm eating today might contain molecules of the original starter from, say, Noah's wife.

A more troubling concern popped into my mind. What if I had a bag of four-day-old starter, plus another one from last week, and a third bag of glop walked in the door? I'd need a special app to keep track of which one to squeeze and which one to stir (*do not* use a metal spoon).

And what if I accidentally made the bread on day nine? Would the loaf pan hold my oven hostage for twenty-four hours? Worse, what if I didn't get around to tossing in the baking power until day twelve? Would the bowl turn into a small nuclear device?

Then I saw a note at the bottom of the recipe and sighed with relief: "This bread is forgiving. If you miss a few days, just squeeze daily until you can bake it."

Hmm. That's precisely the recipe I'd been using to keep my friendships going: a quick squeeze and a "Catch you later!" and off I went to hang out in other kitchens.

What I needed was God's recipe for friendship, with ingredients like honesty, compassion, and loyalty. And patience. Even when a friend is having a bad day and needs to whine. Even when she's having a great day and wants to brag.

Friendship means shared laughter, shared tears, shared opinions: "The pleasantness of a friend springs from their heartfelt advice" (Prov. 27:9 NIV). And yes, like homemade bread, friendships require a generous measure of forgiveness. For postponed lunches and missed birthdays and forgotten promises. For things we wish we'd said, and things we wish we hadn't.

Sometimes the best friendships get off to a messy start. Just keep squeezing, add the right ingredients, and let it bake until done. Delicious.

A friend loves at all times.

Proverbs 17:17 NIV

the supper club

an experiment in community

dawn camp

Do you feel a little desperate for a girls' night out sometimes? Me too. Sometimes I casually tell my girlfriends that I'd love a night out, but inside I know something's gotta give. It's natural to crave friendship: sitting around a table together eating and chatting recharges our batteries.

That's how the email began, the one that I sent to twenty-some ladies earlier this month in an attempt to start a monthly Sunday night supper club. This idea had gently brewed in my mind for a couple of months but only gathered steam when I read about Shauna Niequist's monthly cooking club in her book *Bread & Wine: A Love Letter to Life around the Table*.

Throughout the email I sprinkled quotes from *Bread & Wine*, such as, "People aren't longing to be impressed; they're longing to feel like they're home," and outlined a plan for incorporating monthly themes, like:

book club/what's on your nightstand

writing cards of encouragement

arts and crafts (teach us something or let's create together)

what your dreams are

sharing your story

favorite things party/gift exchange

I didn't know how many ladies would come, but I couldn't let myself worry about that. (It's easy to waste time worrying

about numbers, isn't it?) Ultimately, I trusted that the ladies who needed to be there would come.

On that first Sunday night, four of us sat down for over three hours and ate and talked and laughed. It was wonderful. I had asked everyone to be prepared to share the book or blog or magazine they're currently reading (you'll never guess what I chose), but we talked so much about life in general that we completely forgot.

Lately I've been thinking more deeply about hospitality, friendship, support, shared experience, and moments lived around a table. I don't know what will become of our supper club—if it was a one-time event or if others will want to host—but I know that *I can't do without my girlfriends, and sweet moments shared are worth taking the time to plan and savor.*

Friendship is acting out God's love for people in tangible ways.

Shauna Niequist, *Cold Tangerines*

friendship

a piece of cake

ann swindell

𝓘 have spent most of my life being the pursuer in female friendships. In junior high and high school, I was the one who always invited girlfriends over to my house. In college, I was the one who invited other women to coffee dates. Even now, as a mom, I am the one in our circle of friends who plans the get-togethers most of the time. The other day, when I mentioned scheduling another dinner, one of my friends laughingly responded, "I was just thinking to myself—Ann needs to organize another girls' night!"

And I don't mind it. Really. I'm outgoing, proactive, social. I like bringing women together and helping to create a space in which we can rest, reflect, and laugh together. It's important. It doesn't happen enough.

But sometimes I forget how special it feels to be pursued by other women in friendship. Last week, I was reminded.

My husband is a pastor, and this past weekend was our college retreat, kicking off on Friday night with dinner at our house. We were expecting about twenty students and leaders to come over and begin the retreat by sharing a meal. Unsurprisingly, I spent a lot of time on Friday prepping for their arrival.

Earlier in the week, my friend Andrea had asked me if she could drop something off on Friday. I hadn't thought much about it, knowing that I would be busy getting the house and food ready. When I opened the door to her knock early on Friday afternoon, she was standing there holding a big slice of cake.

And not just any cake. My favorite flavor from my favorite bakery in town.

She smiled at me, and then she said she knew we had a big weekend coming up and just wanted to "drop a little something off." She told me that she was praying for us.

I enveloped her in a hug and laughed. She had me pegged; chocolate is one of my love languages and a swift way into my heart. More than that, though, I felt loved and known by Andrea. She is a new mom with a job; she is as busy and tired as we all are. But she had taken time out of her day to drive across town, pick up a piece of cake, and then drop it off at my home.

It was a small gesture but it meant a great deal to me. That cake reminded me that Andrea valued our friendship; that she was, in a tangible way, pursuing me.

Maybe you're like me, and you're used to being the pursuer in friendships. My encouragement? Don't stop. Andrea's cake has reminded me that I should continue to pursue the women in my life whom I value as friends. Pursuit deeply matters.

A latte dropped off for a mom whose baby has an ear infection can go a long way. The caffeine will keep her awake, yes, but more importantly the reminder that she's going to make it as a new mom will keep her spirits up. A homemade meal (or a meal lovingly purchased from Chick-fil-A) dropped off when your friend's husband is out of town might give her fifteen minutes of alone time rather than another fifteen minutes standing over the stove. But more than that, it might give her desperately needed encouragement during a week when she's running on empty. Calling a friend to pray with her when she's discouraged, dropping a note in the mail, shooting a quick email—there are many ways to pursue the female friendships in our lives.

If you're not typically the pursuer in friendships, my encouragement is to try. Your phone call or text might be a lifeline one day for a friend who usually seems very bold and put-together.

Because, ultimately, being pursued by a friend tells us that we're not alone. It tells us that we have other women who see us, believe in us, and are able—and willing—to help us. And that is the truth at the core of our faith: we are not alone. Jesus will never leave us nor forsake us, and when we pursue our friends we get to join with Him by being His hands and His presence in their lives.

Sometimes, those hands are holding cake.

All you need is love. But a little chocolate now and then doesn't hurt.

Charles M. Schulz (attributed)

the value of "i'm sorry"

karina allen

This surprise apology happened just this past week. My sweet friend Sarah and I have been friends for about five years. We went to church together and went on mission trips to Mexico. Like many friends, we eventually drifted apart. She was in school and had a boyfriend. After she graduated, she got married and for the last couple of years had been moving around the country. I have always kept up with her travels on Facebook but we have not had face-to-face quality time in years. Even though Sarah and her husband had moved back to Baton Rouge a few months ago, we still hadn't connected.

Then, last Thursday, Sarah announced on Facebook that they were moving again, to San Diego. I commented simply to ask her when she was moving. Her response caught me totally off guard. She said, "Probably not until August. We need to hang out! I've been moving around so much that I haven't kept in touch with you! Sorry for that!" I must admit that I got a little teary eyed. Even as I write now, I am tearing up.

Sarah infused my spirit with such value and love and care and thoughtfulness with that apology. Often, when friends move away there is a fear that you will be forgotten because they have gone on to their new lives. There is a strong sense of feeling left behind. I was not expecting an apology nor did I think that I was in need of one. But somewhere inside I needed to know that she hadn't forgotten me, that I *mattered*. Sarah's apology spoke volumes! It went far beyond her regret that we had not kept in touch. It spoke of her love for me and my importance to her even though we are in different seasons and are often separated by distance.

Apologies are complicated. They can be for something small or something big. We just need to be aware that what we have said or done or haven't said or haven't done has had an impact on someone else. When we are sensitive to the Holy Spirit, He will show us just how much influence we possess. God's desire for us is to always be reconciled to the community that we are a part of. That is what paves the way for us to worship God in Spirit and truth.

Everyone wants to be loved. Everyone wants to be acknowledged. Everyone wants to be remembered. Everyone wants to be valued. An apology holds that power and so much more!

Ah, how good it feels! The hand of an old friend.

Henry Wadsworth Longfellow,
The New-England Tragedies

what scares me most

joy forney

Of all the things I was scared of about moving to Africa, what scared me most might surprise you. Well, okay, snakes are an obvious one, but I've had plenty of time living with snakes, so that is nothing new.

But really? My greatest fear?

Making friends.

Yeah. Not Ebola, or malaria, or riots, or bombs, or terrorists. Friends. (Who said I was deep?) Let me be honest. Girls scare me. Ever since first grade, I have been a little leery of girl friendships. And frankly, it took a lot of time and growing and learning about myself to develop close friends while we were living in Indonesia. Eight years on a small team and I was just beginning to feel comfortable with my friendships. And then God said, *How about Uganda?* (He likes to keep me on my toes.) Gulp.

I don't want to be the new girl.

So there we were in Uganda, settling in, and someone I've met a few times invited me to a monthly book club. I love books. I love discussing books. If you've met me in real life, you know this. Usually you can't get away from a conversation with me without hearing the question, "What are you reading?"

So I said yes. And then I panicked. A whole room full of women I don't know? I wanted to back out, stay home, get in my jammies, and watch *Blue Bloods* with my hubby. It is safer to avoid the insecurity, the awkward feelings. I know this about myself.

However, I really did, deep down, want to go, not only to discuss books but to make friends. So I told my husband, my daughter, and a friend in Indonesia not to, under any circumstances, let me back out from going. And when it came time, I hemmed and hawed and made excuses—and they shoved me out the door. I got myself into the car and drove myself there, shaking the whole way. I went.

And you know what? I had a nice time. It was fun to chat about books and enjoy some wine and cheese. I even found a few familiar faces in the group. I'm proud of myself for not backing out. I am still finding my way and making friends. Moving to a new place can be lonely, and I am trying to do my part by showing up and choosing to be my authentic self.

And what am I finding in the midst of the awkwardness? Am I leaning into God and seeing what He has to teach me in this season? Or am I too consumed by my selfish insecurity to see His plan in all of it?

God is the truest and dearest friend, and I'm learning to lean into Him during awkward and lonely times (see Lam.

3:22–23; Rom. 8:35). He wraps me in His everlasting arms and tells me I am His beloved daughter. And I wonder if that wasn't His plan all along—to take me out of my comfort zone so I could experience a deeper and sweeter communion with Him, and to conform me to His Son.

> For those whom he foreknew he also predestined to be conformed to the image of his Son, in order that he might be the firstborn among many brothers.
>
> Romans 8:29 ESV

So what scares me most? Yes, girls scare me, but I am more afraid of missing the beautiful grace God wants to show me in the uncomfortable.

God will take you where you haven't intended to go in order to produce in you what you could not achieve on your own. You know what the Bible calls that? Grace.

> Paul Tripp, "The Theology
> of Uncomfortable Grace"

the importance of face-to-face girlfriends

dawn camp

Online relationships can be satisfying, an easily accessible source of support in our day-to-day lives. Thanks to Facebook, I connect with childhood friends, out-of-state family, even my sixth-grade teacher. In many ways, the internet has changed the face of friendship. But as easy as these connections are to maintain, I encourage you to build meaningful, face-to-face, God-honoring friendships.

I understand the temptation to live online. My online friends don't know how messy my house is or when my roots need retouching. You don't see the extra pounds I've put on this winter, when I yell at my kids, or the look of disappointment on my husband's face when I stay up late to finish writing a blog post instead of going to bed.

You see what I allow you to see, and I promise, it's been Photoshopped.

My online friends often share interests that those around me don't. I love that. Still, there are times when I want to walk away from my online identity, delete my blog, and run away. Writing a post that I think is good but doesn't get comments, stepping outside my comfort zone to ask for a conference sponsorship and not getting a response, being bitten by the comparison bug—there will always be someone who does what I do better than me.

Online interactions may be long-distance, but they can still leave you feeling exposed and vulnerable. That's why I need my real-life girlfriends who share my day-to-day joys and sorrows: the laughs, the tears, the high fives. We share a common history and a stash of inside jokes.

Here are tips for building face-to-face relationships that work.

One: develop friendships that build up your family, not tear it down. In Proverbs 14:1 we're told that "Every wise woman buildeth her house: but the foolish plucketh it down with her hands." My best friends and I love a girls' night out, but we also get together sometimes as couples or families. Four of my dearest friends and I recently took a mother/daughter retreat, which strengthened our daughters spiritually and deepened the bonds of our friendships and families. And our husbands know that we support each other's marriages and would never say or do anything to harm them.

Two: we all need friends with whom we can ponder the deep questions and share our hopes and fears. My strongest friendships are with my church sisters, the ones with whom

87

I share the precious bond of faith. It can still be scary baring my deepest thoughts, but I trust them and we share a Christian worldview.

Three: real friends allow you to let your hair down and just be silly. On the way out of town for a girlfriends' weekend, three friends and I stopped at a charming mountain restaurant with live music. Giddy about our trip, we actually talked our waitress into taking a photo of us on stage with the husband/wife band who performed. I'm sure we'll laugh about it for years!

As a blogger, I seek a comfortable balance between my online and face-to-face friendships. I doubt my girlfriends and I will ever discuss search engine optimization, social networking, what to wear to blog conferences, or a host of other issues and geekery that I adore discussing online. On the other hand, they'll be there for a girls' night out when my week has been lousy and my pageviews are low, whether they understand what that means or not.

I treasure both kinds of friends.

The better part of one's life consists of his friendships.

Abraham Lincoln, "Letter to Joseph Gillespie, July 13, 1849"

hospitality

Hospitality isn't about inviting people into our perfect homes, it's about inviting them into our imperfect hearts.

Edie Wadsworth, *31 Days to a Heart of Hospitality*

just jump in

tsh oxenreider

One of the hardest things about the culture where I lived in the Middle East was the definition of cleanliness. See, no matter how clean I thought our home was (not that it was ever spotless, with two preschoolers underfoot), it paled in comparison to my average neighbor's home.

My local friends—when they cleaned, they *cleaned*. There was hardly a time I saw a dust bunny in their homes—and to boot, it was an honor if you dropped by unannounced. Swinging by to say hello usually turned into a two-hour tea, complete with pastries and undivided attention.

And if you're doing the math, then yep, giving me honor was to swing by my place unannounced. Where I lived with little people. In a culture that values cleanliness.

Needless to say, it made me nervous.

But you know what I learned? Rarely was there a time I wasn't loved because our house wasn't clean enough. Even if my home was a disaster compared to their pristine dwellings, my local friends never said a word. They just smiled. And loved. And usually laughed at my language blunders.

I've taken this to heart and carried it with me as we've traveled to myriad homes. It's not easy, mind you, but slowly, slowly, I'm chipping away at my perfectionism and learning to not wait to invite friends over for dinner because my home isn't perfectly organized. Or dusted. Or less sticky. Or bigger.

Community and hospitality are about relationships.

It's not about impressing one another. It's not about one-upping each other, sizing each other up, or wringing your hands with worry about what the other person thinks.

It's about being yourself and seeing what happens. As I've set up home over the past decade, I've come to just jump right in and meet new people. I can't wait for the longtime residents to realize I don't know anybody—I'm the one who needs to say hi. *And I've learned to be okay with that.*

Be not forgetful to entertain strangers: for thereby some have entertained angels unawares.

Hebrews 13:2

lessons in hospitality from my hairstylist

melissa michaels

Every six weeks my hairstylist invites me to sit down as she offers me a cup of coffee. Then she carefully wraps a towel around my shoulders and we start talking about what is new since we last spoke. We chat about everyday life at home. We share the challenges of picking paint colors, creating art for the walls, and arranging our homes to work for our families. We laugh about being the type who would probably clean the house for a housekeeper, if we had one. We talk about how we love to invite others into our homes and churches and how we love to make the experience special and meaningful.

We confess to each other that if you stop in our houses on short notice, our heart is to welcome you into the imperfectly lovely, everyday chaos of pets and family. But when we invite you over, we will enjoy blessing you with a special evening that might include a clean (enough) house, good smelling candles, and a simple but pretty table set for you to enjoy as we sit down to get to know each other over a simple but tasty dinner.

It is wonderful to find a kindred spirit who understands me so well, a friend I can talk to and share life with—one who conveniently also happens to make my hair prettier at the same time.

As I tip my head backward into the sink filled with warm, sudsy water and shut my eyes, I start to relax and I take a deep breath. We talk about more than just homes. We share our faith, talk about our work and families, our churches, and ways we can bless and impact others around us.

As she washes away my growing number of gray hairs with the promise of a beautiful new auburn color, we take off the masks and let down our guard and laugh about all the things only your hairdresser knows about you. We share our attempts to stay young while admitting we are not feeling as young as we used to be. We confess how hard it is to adjust to being moms of teens and young adults and the ups and downs of navigating marriage in midlife years.

As she snips away at my hair, trying to shape it into something more presentable, we talk about cutting out extra things from our lives and the challenges we face along the way. We talk about the sacrifice of loving and ministering to broken people and what it means to be the hands and feet of Jesus. We continue to chat while chunks of my hair fall to the ground and more pieces of our hearts are revealed. We talk about letting go of our old ways, striving for growth, being changed, and what God is doing to reshape us as women.

Most of what we talk about comes back to the heart of sharing our lives and the love of God with others. She dries my hair, sprays on some shine, and finally I feel like I am ready to walk back out into the world refreshed and much less frazzled looking than when I walked in. As I schedule my next appointment we exchange words of excitement about what God will do next in our lives. She sends me off with a wave and a smile, and off I go, ready to tackle the rest of my day.

It becomes clear as I head back to my car that my hairstylist-turned-friend practices gracious and heartfelt hospitality, right there in the salon. While we both love sharing our lives with others through opening our homes, hospitality is a matter of the heart. Hospitality is setting the tone for relationships more than it is about the actual place the relationships are formed. I've never been in my hairstylist's home and she has never been in mine. While opening our homes or preparing meals are gifts we can and should offer to those God places in our lives, what matters more is that we serve others by opening our hearts to show interest in people. Our desire should be to make people feel welcomed and loved no matter where our paths cross.

Perhaps our end goal with everyone we meet should be to send them back out into the world a little less frazzled, a little more understood, and feeling noticeably more loved and lovely so they are encouraged and excited to see what God is up to next in their life! That is the true gift of hospitality.

Kindred spirits alone do not change with the changing years.

L. M. Montgomery, *Anne of the Island*

the power of the imperfect

myquillyn smith

Well, I've figured it out.

I've said it a majillion times. I truly believe that the imperfections in our homes have the ability to help put people at ease. There's something about walking in a house and being greeted by a kind person who lives beautifully within her imperfect home, without apology, that makes me want to be friends with her and tell her all my secrets. Why would I want to try to pretend that my home is perfect when imperfection can be so powerful? When I walk into a home, I find myself scanning for something, asking myself, *Is this house too perfect? Too put together? Too unapproachable?* Because if it is, I'm not nearly as comfortable.

Funny, the secret to taking friendship from surface to deep is the same. We already know it; we just wish there was another way. It's simple and nearly impossible all at the same time. We have to show our junk, share the crud, let others know about our imperfections before we can move deeper into friendship.

We've got to show our ugly. It's the only way.

And just like any risk, the best way is to start small. Take a baby step and share a little something personal and see how your friend reacts. Do they listen? Do they encourage? Do they accept you? If so, you are laying the groundwork for a stronger friendship, and most of the time the other person will start sharing their less-than-perfects too. And you build from there. It's risky. All good things are. But friends are worth it.

Maybe you have some friends whom you are wishing you were closer with. Dare to be an imperfectionist.

My friends have made the story of my life. In a thousand ways they have turned my limitations into beautiful privileges.

Helen Keller, *The Story of My Life*

how we can pursue hospitality

jennifer dukes lee

This is my friend Helmer.

He's an old farmer who lives up the road from us. If you drove from our farm to his, you'd pass by the country church where we worship together on Sunday mornings.

There are a lot of things I love about Helmer.

The way he sings hymns by heart—all four verses.

The way he carries a comb in his front pocket.

The way he and his sister, Hazel, take care of each other. (Both in their nineties, they now live together in Helmer's house.)

The way that Helmer likes to keep things simple.

When I need a shift in perspective about life, well, I pay Helmer and Hazel a visit. They keep the main thing, the main thing—devoid of the nonessentials.

Awhile back, I drove the familiar road between our two houses, past the church and the harvested fields. Like I often do, I brought my notebook and a pen, and I scribbled notes while sitting on a sofa between those two sages.

Then it was time to go.

But before I could leave, Helmer rose from the couch in a bit of a rush. Soon, plates and cups clinked. I knew he was setting a table, but I felt short on time.

I peeked around the corner to protest. Sure enough, Helmer had set out "lunch," which in our part of the world is shorthand for a small midafternoon snack.

But lunch would require us to sit. Lunch is not a grab-and-go activity. It's a linger-at-the-table event.

Mind you, Helmer didn't complicate matters. That's not his style. This was it:

Three cups of hot coffee

A small plate of Oreos

And an extra place at the table, for me

I tried to wave him off, told him I needed to get back home. But . . . oh then, well. Sure.

Helmer insisted, and I acquiesced.

The old farmer with a comb in his front pocket led us in prayer: "Come, Lord Jesus. Be our guest. Let these gifts to us be blessed. Amen."

We nibbled on Oreos. We blew our breath over the tops of our cups to cool our coffee. We talked about the weather and the news. About God and the church. And crops.

I left an hour later than I'd planned, but felt surprisingly unrushed. Instead I felt a warmness, a lightheartedness, an awareness of my breathing—the way one feels after a particularly satisfying, winsome day.

Later, I thought about what those hours with Helmer and Hazel have taught me about the nuances of hospitality.

1. Hospitality is insistent, a pursuit.

In some translations, Romans 12:13 has a palpable zeal: "Pursue hospitality" (HCSB). This hospitality is actually quite aggressive. The Greek is saying to chase hospitality. To run hard after it. To actually trouble people about it! (I can almost imagine Helmer's photo on the pages of the Greek dictionary, plate of Oreos in hand.)

2. Hospitality requires a guest.

Sometimes the most hospitable thing we can do is to stay. We say yes to the table set before us. Hospitality is a relationship between a host and a guest. Surely, every good thing in life can be improved by sharing it with another soul. And if we don't acquiesce from time to time, we disallow the gift being offered.

3. Hospitality is about human dignity.

At the heart of hospitality is the simple act of opening a space, of making room. It is a quiet acknowledgment of the automatic sacredness of another human being's life. It's the easy dignity of sharing a table.

4. Hospitality doesn't need a tablescape.

Hospitality doesn't need matching napkins or three-course meals. It doesn't require Pinterest's help.

Sometimes, it's only this—

One old farmer who sets out a cup
And lets you know you matter because you exist
And you can't help but stay awhile

There is no happiness like that of being loved by your fellow creatures, and feeling that your presence is an addition to their comfort.

Charlotte Brontë, *Jane Eyre*

my love language is food

sandy coughlin

My husband and I recently met some new friends. We immediately felt a warmth and connection, a desire to know them more. We've been doing this friendship thing for almost twenty-three years now, forming new bonds with other people together as a couple.

"Going there"—exposing ourselves, becoming vulnerable and known. We all want to be loved, valued, and accepted. It's just how we're wired inside, but for many it's a rough road to get there.

I was thinking this last weekend about how my love language is food. You've probably read about the five ways that people like to experience and give love: words of affirmation, physical touch, quality time, receiving gifts, and acts of service. But for me, I know that food is what I'm all about. *My love language is food.*

And not just the four basic food groups, though I like those a lot. I mean all that food represents. It's more than taste, calories, or sustenance. It's what sitting down and communing with others represents—the somewhat lost art of what it means to get together with others.

My husband and I love to take relationships to the next level through the sharing of a meal. It always involves food.

Getting down to the nitty-gritty, around our dinner table, is the way I can show love and care about people, when gifts and sometimes even words are uncomfortable. It says "I love you" without any physical touch (okay, well, I do often give a hug at the end of the evening). It's a way to bring people together, to love on them, to listen and to nourish, and then when the night is over I will know that I have done my job.

My husband and I have learned to do this together as a couple, but it doesn't always have to be this way. We are individuals and we all have our own passions and ways to show love.

The love language of food is in my DNA. I really do think I was born with it, passed on to me from my parents, especially my mother. It's a gift she gave to me, and I feel that I need to pass it on to others. Another way of "paying it forward."

Hey, do you want to come for dinner?

1. Inviting people. Who should get to know who? Who could benefit by knowing this person, or that couple?
2. Planning the menu. Simplicity is the best form of happiness. Good food can be simple and healthy. Actually, the best is right from the garden.
3. Cooking the food. No long, drawn-out recipes for me. Chop, serve it fresh, grill or broil, and make the plate colorful.
4. Serving the guests. We like to serve; it's just our style. Don't get up, we'll bring it to you.
5. Cleaning up. After they leave, we get our hands deep in the suds, push "start" on the dishwasher, then fall into bed.

We're in deep. Entertaining defines us. When I think of my friends, the ones I want to cultivate deeper friendships with, the ones I find value in and want to get to know more, I can't even imagine not having a meal with them.

You sit, relax, engage, pour your heart out, become authentic and vulnerable, and usually it's mutually pleasurable. You learn pretty quickly from the times that it's not.

The love language of food has a way of bringing down walls, because you're less guarded and more trusting when sharing a meal.

It's innately a trusting act. It truly shows love.

Feeding people is a way of loving them.

Shauna Niequist, *Bittersweet*

how to feel at home in your house and your skin

lisa-jo baker

Sunday afternoons in South Africa—there were always watermelons bopping in the swimming pool.

It was to keep them cool till they could be split for dessert.

But to us kids they were just a challenge to ride, to raft, to water polo between ourselves until a grown-up finally noticed and yelled at us to quit it before we turned the insides into pure pulp.

Sunshine on the watermelons and their green striped skins and our shoulders and legs all gangly and growing up, living large on the hospitality of our parents.

I can still feel the water running down my back from wet hair as we stood dripping around the table under the thatch roof lapa as Dad cut into the melons, slice after juicy slice.

We'd stand and bite and suck and spit seeds, and there were always more people than chairs.

My mom could make an ordinary afternoon an event.

So much goodness dripping down our chins and still feeding my memory tonight—twenty-three years later—in a small rental house in northern Virginia.

It's a long way from my Southern Cross childhood and that swimming pool in Pretoria.

Hospitality as I've grown up has looked different.

I discovered a dirty pot in the microwave last night.

I stood and stared at it. It looked like it was from yesterday's tacos. "Pete," I ask over my shoulder. "Did you know there's a pot in the microwave?"

There's a pause before my husband answers.

And then his laughter rolls back from the couch with his words, "Yeah, I guess that's where I hid it before they came over."

I wonder if my mom ever did that? Shoved dirty dishes in the oven or a cupboard? I don't remember us having a microwave.

We've had a lot of guests pass through our conveniently located right-outside-DC house. My desire to host with the carefree abandon of my childhood has gone head-to-head with my desperate self-consciousness about how small our home is.

How the size of our house has felt like it stunted the size of our life.

How pockmarked our yard is with the holes of busy boys, the mud they've lovingly smeared as "cement" all over the back pavement, the rakes and hammers and shovels and old gloves they've forgotten in piles around their precious "work site" that I don't have the heart to complain about.

How we only have four dining room chairs and the table is littered with markings that even Mr. Clean's Magic Eraser can't seem to remove. And how inevitably my kids will open the hamster's cage and bring him over to the table right as I'm trying to serve the meal.

This used to give me profound waves of panic. Because there's nothing like seeing your house through someone else's eyes to realize the carpet might actually be beyond cleaning.

Or that the toilet seat with the one loose side that never bothers you is an embarrassment when you think about someone else using it. And that if you don't warn the friend helping you load the dishwasher she won't know that you can only pull the rack out so far before it comes completely off the rails and glasses and bottles bounce foolishly off the tracks.

Last weekend one of my oldest friends and her good man, who has been deployed more than he's been home the last few years, and their three kids came to visit. They came several days earlier than we expected.

And there it was. The choice. *Panic or delight.*

Fear of appearances or fully opening my arms to one of my favorite friends. *Picking up the backyard or inviting her boys to join the well-loved chaos.* Stressing over the stains or surrounding ourselves with toys, kids, and enough time to catch up. *Frantically planning something to cook or ordering pizza and slicing a watermelon.*

After five years in this small house with all the brown paneling, I've learned a lot about big hospitality. And no matter how much you clean or remodel or move or rebuild, hospitality will always be more a matter of the heart than the architecture.

109

And your guests will only feel as comfortable in your house as you feel in your own skin. And there's no shame in paper plates if they're heaped high with delight in each other's company. And kids are great role models when it comes to the unselfconscious art of explaining the ins and outs of each other's toilets.

And no one ever did actually die of embarrassment.

But missing out on community is a type of dying, and what if I'd said no to catching up on two decades and three kids since we shared a dorm together?

So it's later, after we've said a hundred goodbyes in the space of ten minutes and the boys have all agreed they'd like to be brothers and next-door neighbors and I've wiped down sticky counters, chairs, and sofas, that I discover that pot in the microwave.

And think about how my mom used to burn the beans because she wasn't paying attention, or run out of mashed potatoes because the kids helped themselves to too much, or flip the brown sofa cushion over to hide where it had split its guts right open.

But she always opened the door.

She always pulled out one more chair.

Kids were always included in the charades, the impromptu Bible lessons, the cleaning up.

And there was always watermelon for dessert.

I'm so thankful for friendship. It beautifies life so much.

L. M. Montgomery, *Anne of Avonlea*

friendship on purpose

No friendship is an accident.
O. Henry, *Heart of the West*

the messy and beautiful in-between

katie kenny phillips

Our relationship reminds me a bit of my fourth grade science project. Two cups propped up against a winter's kitchen window, connected by a single string. Simple, really. Those two cups, each containing their own drops of coloring, standing side by side waiting for change, as life continued around them. Ups and downs. Breakfasts, lunches, dinners. Almost-spills. Worry and work and play. No kitchen windowsill is immune, because everywhere seconds become minutes and minutes become hours and things happen and things always change. And I watched the space in between on that windowsill, the blending of colors and the growing and the string becoming more than just fibers but something crystalizing into something else entirely. The in-between was mysterious and surprising and exactly what it was meant to be. Connected by a string—those cups—day after day, something beautiful was *becoming*.

Her name, *Crystal*, reminds me of that windowsill project and of our friendship. It reminds me of how God grew us together in our own in-betweens by drawing on our individual colors and time. He grew something beautiful from two women connected by the One who knew exactly what would become of our string as the seconds became minutes became soul-sister friendship.

God brought us together after a long while of just bumping into each other. We spent years sitting very far apart on that kitchen windowsill—not really connecting except for occasional hellos and a genuine appreciation for one another. It wasn't until she was in the beginning stages of leaving the country with her family to do mission work and I was in the beginning stages of health problems with one of my kids, and then on to the even longer journey of foster care and adoption, that God surprisingly thrust us together—gently connecting us by a small but sturdy string—and something, *something*, started growing.

We each felt like wanderers on an unexpected and terrifying journey, and we locked hands and held up each other's arms and muddled through the desert together.

It was in the middle of our unknowns where we found each other. Often we'd find ourselves crying over something that seemed impossible and we'd sniffle into loose, crumpled napkins from our purses. Or we'd secretly laugh when we admitted our fears—that once whispered aloud in the confines of her office actually sounded ridiculous. We'd drink similar coffees and finish each other's sentences and marvel at how *this* was the time when God would build something together between us. We'd talk about us as kids, as teenagers, as moms, and as

wives. Growth often took place while we prepared Bible studies together or hashed out events or topics that would occur in our church. Now that she is far away on the mission field, our friendship grows through texts sent in the middle of breakfast or while folding laundry, in the middle of the ordinary stuff that makes up seconds and minutes and hours and lives. It seemed to us that our friendship should've happened years before so we would've had more time together. But God knew the timing for us, in order to make it beautiful according to His purpose. We looked up at the right moment and realized we were sisters.

Not that long ago I texted in the late hours of my night and early hours of hers: "I found out that our birth mom might be pregnant again. We most likely will get this baby— and I'm happy. But I feel utterly helpless to protect my little one. Will you join me in praying complete protection over this child? My heart is so heavy. And I can't even tell people about it. How do I express the joy of a future baby mixed with the pain I feel for the momma and with my fear? I feel like God has asked me to look total brokenness and despair in the face and hold it tightly to me."

And she understands. She looks brokenness and despair in the face daily as well, and she knows. She names the child instantly: "Baby Fearfully Made." What she's really doing is naming my pain and joy, and I all but weep for the beauty of it. "Praying all kinds of peace and rescue over that situation," she texts. "I sure do love you." And she sends the Scripture that she has already begun praying over the baby and me. Just like that, she's lifting arms across hours and oceans.

"Baby Fearfully Made" never came to be, and I messaged her when I discovered the news. Relief, disappointment. A thousand other things. Through it all, though, I felt deep gratitude for her friendship because I had begged her to storm the gates of heaven—this time for someone who *didn't even exist*—and she did. She did it immediately and she would and will do it again. And I consider it an honor to storm heaven for her too. We've prayed together before her doctor's appointments, during tests, and while she was waiting outside without shoes as she was evacuated from a hotel on fire. She sends me messages of things I cannot tell anyone about, but she knows I can handle it because I look brokenness and despair in the face on this continent as well. We're connected by a common, unbreakable string.

I messaged her recently: "I know why I love our friendship. Why do you?" Nothing like opening up your heart to someone and trusting she'll see it for what it is. And her immediate response: "When put on the spot, I can't put my finger on specifics. It's like a Monet painting—all dots up close. But when you stand back, a pretty spectacular masterpiece. Each text, you know, a different dot."

Our friendship looks like that—a masterpiece. Or like a glorious fourth grade science project propped up against a winter's kitchen window, connected by a single string. No matter. It's messy and it's beautiful. In between and to the very end.

True friends are always together in spirit.

L. M. Montgomery,
Anne of Green Gables

she scares me

melanie porter

She scares me," the young lady said as she pointed to a name on the Bible study sign-up sheet. I burst out laughing because the name belonged to a dear friend of mine. This "scary" friend, bold in spirit with a heart as big as Texas, talks with a delightful Tennessee twang, making her seem a little rough around the edges. I could see how this young lady might be intimidated by my friend's larger-than-life persona.

I started thinking about all the times we miss out on friendship opportunities because we perceive something different than reality. We shy away because the person seems busy, hateful, haughty, or a myriad of other perceptions.

In all actuality, the quiet lady who sits to your left in worship may be insecure, not haughty. The young mom brushing past you in a hurry may be at the end of her momma rope with three little ones in tow. The shy girl who looks away when you catch her eye may be drowning in grief or depression.

The truth is we all come to the friendship table with hangups and insecurities. We all have broken, raw places. It's not easy to put ourselves out there, but the Bible tells us that in order to have friends, we must show ourselves friendly.

I grew up believing first impressions were lasting impressions, especially in the professional world. However, Christians should have a different view simply based on God's reply to Samuel when seeking the new king of Israel: "The LORD does not look at the things people look at. People look

at the outward appearance, but the LORD looks at the heart" (1 Sam. 16:7 NIV).

How about we start taking time to get to know the hearts belonging to all those new faces? What if we extend grace?

Everyone has bad days and no one is immune to letting emotions slip in hasty replies. The beautiful lady dressed to the hilt with all the diamonds might be the most humble person in the room. The chatty girl may not be annoying once you get to know her and realize her infectious zeal for life.

Given the opportunity to engage my "scary" friend, the young lady soon fell in love with her. This experience encouraged me to take off my blinders of perception and be bold in showing myself friendly.

Why not be the one to step out and extend the hand of friendship? What do you have to lose? You never know what God has waiting for you on the other side of a friendly conversation.

For God hath not given us the spirit of fear; but of power, and of love, and of a sound mind.

2 Timothy 1:7

cantaloupe wisdom

joanne kelly

*I*t was just a quick stop at the grocery store—a handbasket, produce-department-only kind of stop.

I stepped through the doors, grabbed the blue-handled basket from the stack so well positioned by a smart store employee. I'm sure I'm not the only woman who run-walks through a store—it's an "I know what I'm doing and what I'm here for" approach to supermarket stops, and I'm positive I've bumped into others with the same mindset. I headed through the unnecessary take-out food section and approached the area of conveniently precut, well-displayed fruits and veggies. I rarely buy the already diced veggies for my stir-fries and salads. I am always happy to do that myself. But the fruit is different. There's something about seeing the inside of fruit that helps me know it's going to taste as good as I want it to.

If anyone ever masters the skill of whole watermelon picking, I need to learn from you. I'm disappointingly wrong more than fifty percent of the time.

Reaching into the cool shelves, I pushed aside some of the watermelon pieces that looked less tasty. The well-dressed elderly woman to my left straightened slightly from her cantaloupe search to see who was joining her. As she looked at me, I noticed that she had on a melon-colored jacket and matching lipstick that I'm sure she had carefully chosen for her shopping occasion. She looked to be about eighty years old or more—a very well-kept, beautiful woman, but most definitely older than my mother.

"I used to buy that for my husband," she told me as she watched me rearrange the containers of watermelon pieces. "I don't buy it anymore. There is always too much for just me to eat."

I learned very quickly that she no longer had her husband to share life with. Amazing how much you can learn about someone while choosing fruit.

I told her I like to buy cut pieces so I can see how ripe it is, and also knowing it will all get eaten quickly with no mushy leftovers. I suggested she might try buying a smaller piece for herself—no waste to worry about.

She smiled and started looking through the plastic-wrapped watermelon with me.

"That's a good idea. I do like it. My husband liked it more . . ."

Her pleasant voice trailed off and I couldn't make out everything she said. Or maybe my mind trailed off, thinking about what it would be like in the twilight years of my life to go on without my soul mate. It's obvious their preferences live on in us, even in the produce section, and will always remain a part of us.

"And this is good for your face."

I turned to her again as she held out a neatly wrapped half-cantaloupe.

"For my face?" I came back to our conversation.

"It's good for your skin. It gives a glow and helps fight against wrinkles." She smiled at me.

I knew she knew.

This would be one of those facts that I didn't even want to double-check with Google. I had no idea if she ever worked in the skin care profession, or even kept track of how many wrinkles she had not gained due to her intake of cantaloupe. Maybe her husband had been a dermatologist. But I doubt it. And it didn't matter. The simple fact that she had lived life beyond what I had made her an expert on some things I knew very little about.

I couldn't help but think of Titus:

Guide older women into lives of reverence so they end up as neither gossips nor drunks, but models of goodness. By looking at them, the younger women will know how to love their husbands and children, be virtuous and pure, keep a good house, be good wives. We don't want anyone looking down on God's Message because of their behavior.

Titus 2:3–5 Message

Whichever side of the exchange you are on at any particular moment of life, there's invaluable stuff to be gleaned from an older, wiser woman. Most of our lives we're lucky enough to be on both sides—older than some, younger than others. My encounter with the lady wearing the melon-colored suit happened on the way to my lunch with a young mom twenty years younger than me.

Life is full of taking in and giving out—sometimes without even realizing it.

By the time I had selected the correct watermelon, I turned to see my elderly advice-giver busy sorting through the abundant contents of her shopping cart. She had added a lovely thin wedge of pink watermelon to her stash, and I a bright half-cantaloupe to mine.

I like to imagine she enjoyed her sweet fruit, reliving joyful summer memories of her husband, and I like to imagine I may have a more glowing, wrinkle-free complexion in the days to come. I gained a lot more from that quick stop than my handbasket could hold.

There's not a word yet, for old friends who've just met.

Jim Henson, *Favorite Songs from Jim Henson's Muppets*

the one quality of great and generous minds

edie wadsworth

The boys were home this past weekend and so we lingered awhile around the table, talking about their first couple weeks in classes and all the myriad adjustments to be made when you begin a new season of life. One thing that can be hard is all the new people that begin to populate your life, which can also be overwhelming. I confessed to them how hard that can be even at my stage of life, even though I'm an extrovert and love meeting people.

I was at a social gathering recently and I wasn't feeling that well and wasn't really in a curious or generous mood. I wanted to enjoy my expensive dinner and read the book I had stowed away in my purse and pretend I was eating alone. *I have enough friends,* I told myself. *And this woman across from me is twenty years my senior and she's not talkative, so this is going to be a monumental effort to make genuine conversation.*

But then I remembered what I always tell my kids. Teach yourself to be interested in people, to want to hear their stories. And if you're not interested, confess that as a flaw in yourself and pretend to be interested until your stubborn mind catches up.

I think we're not that curious about other people because we have to stop thinking and talking about ourselves long enough to let them talk. It takes humility—which C. S. Lewis says is not thinking less of yourself, but thinking of yourself less. And we are nothing if not hopelessly self-centered, so this humility and curiosity don't come natural to any of us—least of all, me.

So, despite my own selfish thoughts, I started asking this woman questions. Twenty minutes later I was sure she was one of the most fascinating women I had ever met. I'm so glad I didn't miss that opportunity, but it makes me wonder how many people I've let slip through my fingers because I was too self-absorbed to care.

I told the boys, and I keep reminding myself, to stay curious—to cultivate the discipline of being interested in people. Even if you're not. Even if you already have enough friends. Even when it's inconvenient. Soon it will become more like habit, and years later you'll find that what you've cultivated is a generous heart.

True humility is not thinking less of yourself; it is thinking of yourself less.

C. S. Lewis, *Mere Christianity*   125

when god surprises you

jessica turner

In high school I dated a boy named Greg. He was my first love and a big reason I know the Lord. I loved his family and we made a lot of great memories together. Ultimately, though, we weren't right for each other, and after two years Greg wisely ended the relationship.

I believe God often brings people into our lives for finite pieces of time. Greg was a huge part of my life when I was sixteen, but obviously not anymore. We live in different parts of the country, are both happily married to other people, and have had very little contact in recent years.

And now, fifteen years later, I look back on that time fondly, knowing that God was preparing my heart for the deep love I have found within marriage. Little did I know that He was also preparing the way for a rich friendship to bloom more than a decade later.

You see, about a year ago I received a Facebook message from Greg's older brother, Rob. He was a doctor now, married with a young daughter, and amazingly working at the same health care institution I work for in Nashville. In his note he said, "My wife, Katie, is awesome, and I think you two would really hit it off."

He was right.

Katie has become one of my dearest friends. We love doing life together, and our kids are the best of friends. We cook and share meals. We craft. We change diapers and wipe runny noses. We paint and plan parties. We share Target deals (a very important part of friendship!). We worship together at church.

Katie shines Jesus brightly.

When I take time to sit back and think about how this friend came to be in my life, I am blown away by the workings of God. He didn't just bring a high school sweetheart into my life who helped lead me to Him—which would have been plenty.

No.

Fifteen years later, He brought a dear friend into my life who I would have never known without first knowing Greg. And not just a "let's have coffee once" sort of friend, but a soul sister.

We serve a God of surprises. In my life I have seen God surprise in many ways, but it is relationships that have the most significance for me. God delights in each of us and He created us as relational beings.

My friendship with Katie is a surprise that continues to bring me to my knees in thanksgiving.

I thank my God upon every remembrance of you.

Philippians 1:3

reunion days

christie purifoy

I've written about my extended family before. These are almost always stories of absence. The cousins we have yet to meet. The grandparents we too rarely hold. Family, for us, is always too much or too little.

> I am a foreigner to my own family,
> a stranger to my own mother's children.
> Psalm 69:8 NIV

Our lives are stretched across too many time zones. My father has always said it is a good thing our country is not any larger because then we would only live farther apart. But with one sister's imminent move to Hawaii, our country has suddenly grown much larger. And we will, indeed, live farther apart.

But summer days are reunion days, and through some miracle of spirit and frequent-flier miles, we come together.

They say absence makes the heart grow fonder, and I have found this to be true. But now I know that absence grows other good fruit. Because the holes in our lives where family might be do not stay empty. These gaps and fissures turn out to be fertile ground for things like hospitality and community. Friendship and adventure. Without family to lean on, we become needy, but these needs are always met.

We come together and discover that we do not have less but so much more. We have family and we have friends. We have family and we have neighbors. We have family and we have our communities. We have family and we have life in abundance.

We have more.

May your deeds be shown to your servants,
your splendor to their children.
Psalm 90:16 NIV

what i learned about friendship from my family

I am overwhelmed by the grace and persistence of my people.

Maya Angelou

friendship through a child's eyes

dawn camp

There are situations I simply don't know how to handle unless I've been there myself. My mother used a walking cane for many years, so I treat people who need them like everyone else, with sensitivity instead of awkwardness. But I didn't know how to comfort a woman who'd miscarried a baby until it happened to me. And my experience with special needs children is limited; subsequently, this is one of those areas where I'm still not particularly comfortable or confident in my ability to say or do the right thing.

Last year a family with a special needs child moved across the street from us. Hannah can't run and play outside with the other kids. She doesn't laugh and tell silly stories. Her mother pushes her in a stroller that supports her head and neck. Did I reach out to this family and befriend this mother and child? No, I'm ashamed to say that in my inadequacy and unfamiliarity with this kind of situation, I did not.

133

A few weeks ago, my three- and five-year-old daughters started going over to Hannah's house to play. Then my seven- and ten-year-old started going too. I have no disillusionment where my children are concerned: I know they are moochers, and will eat any snacks, gum, or popsicles they can get their hands on. I worried they were taking advantage of Hannah's family.

What I didn't see was that they were making friends with a child who couldn't go out and make friends on her own. They go to Hannah's house and paint and play; they tell me funny stories of how she sighs when she doesn't like something and sways with joy when she does. When my seven-year-old daughter described how they dance with Hannah, her body supported in a special walker that holds her almost upright, I was so choked up I could hardly speak.

This morning three of my children accompanied Hannah and her family to a special showing of *Ratatouille* for special needs children and their friends and family. Ironing out the details on the phone yesterday, Hannah's mom told me what a blessing my children's visits have been. This is the first time Hannah has gone to the movies. If all goes well, a trip to Dairy Queen for ice cream will follow. Anticipation of this outing has been one of the highlights of the week in our home.

We all have infirmities. Some are just more visible than others.

We then that are strong ought to bear the infirmities of the weak.

Romans 15:1

a good friend

tina anderson

This morning, I watched two boys tumble out of the backseat of my car and scramble toward the school. Their backpacks bounced wildly as they ran and playfully shoved each other off the sidewalk. I couldn't hear them, but I knew that they were giggling and calling each other out with mock indignation, "Duuude!?"

Since the day I knew I was pregnant, I have prayed for many things for my child, but my constant prayer has been that he would be blessed with a good friend. As I watched the two boys disappear around the corner, I sensed that, for this season at least, my prayer had been answered.

When I say "a good friend" I don't mean someone who enjoys the same things he does or someone who will reciprocate playdates. What I want for Sean is a friend who possesses the biblical quality of goodness—a good friend. Proverbs 17:17 says, "A friend loves at all times" (ESV) and a friend

who loves at all times does not let his buddy do something that would make his mommy sad.

And in Bryan, Sean's BFF for this season (or, dare I even hope, for life?), I see a boy who has the fruit of goodness growing in him.

Not long ago, Bryan was over to play and Sean was being a real toot. When I took Bryan home, I told him I was sorry that Sean had not been very nice to him and he said—and this blew me away—"That's okay, he's probably just tired."

Grace and goodness—what more could you want in a friend?

Bryan's mother tells me he has his days too (who doesn't?), but on the whole, I see in him an innate desire to do what is good and right. He is a boy who is cautious and doesn't like getting in trouble, and Sean needs someone like that to temper his sometimes dramatic free-spiritedness.

I know that with each passing year, the influence of the world will increase in his life and my influence will decrease. I know that the company he keeps will influence the choices he makes. I know that the stakes only get higher as his world gets bigger. The people he chooses to partner with in friendships along the way will have a hand in writing the story of his life.

I know that the time is coming when I will have to lengthen the rope, to let him go with his friends (clear out of my sight!), and in this letting go he will encounter choices to go left or right. And I think the best I can hope for is that he will have at least one good friend who will hold him accountable, who will be willing to challenge a questionable choice or at least speak up and say, "Dude. Maybe you shouldn't do that."

At some point in life, one has (hopefully) developed some wisdom and discernment, and friends of all sorts are a good thing; I think we are called to that. But for a nine-year-old who has yet to fully develop those traits—right now he needs, and has, a good friend.

And that is an answered prayer.

Iron sharpeneth iron; so a man sharpeneth the countenance of his friend.

Proverbs 27:17   137

give love freely

lisa leonard

esterday, I was walking David to his special needs class-room in the morning when a little boy with autism, about the same age as David, ran up to greet him.

"Good morning, David!" he said with a huge smile on his face. David stopped, looked straight into the little boy's eyes, and smiled back. It was such a sweet moment, I felt my heart bursting in my chest.

Then the little boy bent down closer to David, covered his face with his hands, and then quickly moved them apart, yelling, "Peek-a-boo!"

David's grin got bigger and his eye contact never wavered.

This exchange went on for a few minutes, while I stood by and watched, mouth agape, heart bursting, tears in my eyes.

I was in awe of these little boys, whose bodies are affected by disabilities but whose hearts are whole. They give love freely. They understand each other in a way I can't. They have a soul-ish connection because they've walked through life with bodies that won't cooperate with them. And yet they still have friendship and joy and smiles to give.

I am so thankful I got to witness this moment. I'm thankful I get to learn from them—and to be reminded that having a disability doesn't mean you don't understand how to give love. Perhaps it's enabled them to love more deeply.

I'm thankful that there is beauty to be found in the smallest moments.

And he said unto me, My grace is sufficient for thee: for my strength is made perfect in weakness. Most gladly therefore will I rather glory in my infirmities, that the power of Christ may rest upon me.

2 Corinthians 12:9

when friendship is tough

lysa terkeurst

One of the wisest pieces of advice on friendship I ever got was from one of my daughters.[1] She was in middle school at the time. You know that awkward place where insecurities run rampant, hormones rage, and your best friend one day becomes your worst enemy the next? So lovely.

She got in the car one day with tears filling her eyes. She waited until we pulled out of the school parking lot to let all her hurt leak down her cheeks.

"Rough day?" I asked.

"Awful," she replied.

I turned down the radio, waited until we were at a red light, and reached for her hand. "Wanna talk about it?"

---

1. Lysa TerKeurst, "When Friendship Is Tough," originally published in *Encouragement for Today: Devotions for Everyday Living* by Renee Swope, Lysa TerKeurst, Samantha Evilsizer, and the Proverbs 31 Ministries Team (Grand Rapids: Zondervan, 2013), 31–32.

"Nope," she whispered as she turned her face away from me toward the window.

The rest of the night she sulked around the house. And no matter how many times I tried to get her to talk, this normally very vocal child wouldn't open up. So the next morning, I was surprised when she bounded down the stairs with a smile on her face.

"Well hey! You sure look happy this morning," I said as I lifted up quick thank-you prayers to God for whatever had brought back the sunshine to my girl's life.

"Mom," she said with great authority, "I've decided something about friends. They all have good stuff and bad stuff. Things you like and things that really annoy you. So, you just have to decide if you can handle their package deal."

How wise. How true.

Friends are a package deal. And sadly, not all friendships will stand the test of time. Some friendships are for a season.

But other times, we have to be willing to deal with the messy stuff to fight for our friendships.

Recently, I had something hard happen with a friend I dearly love and greatly respect. A misunderstanding. Hurt feelings. Frustration. Part of me wanted to distance myself because it was hard to sift through the hurt. But as I prayed through it, I had to remind myself this person was a package deal.

Part of what makes her a great friend whom I love being around is her tenacity and passion to accomplish tasks with excellence. But because she is so task-oriented, she is less relationally sensitive. And if I'm honest with myself, I can see that I'm a package deal too. With good stuff. And annoying stuff.

She has issues. I have issues.

We're both messy people, willing to work on our not-so-fun stuff, who are fully aware we're going to hit some muddy little potholes along our friendship path.

But we've decided the package deal is worth it.

Be completely humble and gentle; be patient, bearing with one another in love. Make every effort to keep the unity of the spirit through the bond of peace.

Ephesians 4:2–3 NIV

enjoy the beauty of friendships, no matter how long they last

bonnie gray

There is a special kind of freedom friends enjoy . . . the freedom to simply be themselves.

Willa Cather, as quoted in Rebecca Currington,
*Friendship Is a Blessing: Inspirational
Reflections of Friendship*

J was sipping my coffee, admiring the flowers. I was sitting with my five-year-old son, Josh, to make sure he finished the last bites of his breakfast.

The roses I got for Mother's Day were opening up beautifully, but their blossoms were starting to shed on the table.

"Why do flowers die?" Josh asked.

Philosophy at seven in the morning caught me by surprise.

"What do you mean?" I answered, buying myself some time.

"There's water in the vase. How come they're not alive?"
I tried to figure how best to explain biology to Mr. Curious, but I decided to take a different route.

"Water keeps them alive until the flower blooms," I said. "Then the petals fall off and they are done being flowers."

"That's so sad," Josh replied.

A New Vision

I've felt the same about some friendships. *I thought true friendship was forever. Didn't I handle it with enough care? Why did it end?*

It's hard to trust again after you've been hurt. For the longest time, it felt safer to serve others and soldier on emotionally alone. It's interesting to me—the more I retreated, the more my heart ached. Although I wanted to protect myself, I longed to trust again.

As I prayed for a new vision for friendship, God brought some beautiful pictures to mind.

Friendship, as I've come to learn, *isn't a possession.*

Friendship is more like *God's beauty found in nature.*

The Beauty of Friendship

We can appreciate friendship like we do—

A beautiful sunset. You can never re-create the sky you once saw across the desert at twilight. You enjoy it while it lasts. These are moments where you connect with a friend, but life takes you on different paths.

A *shooting star.* Some friends seem to appear out of nowhere, when our journeys go through dark times. Like a shooting star, someone offers the space to be heard and to be known. They bring special encouragement, refreshing us just in one moment of need.

Flowers in bloom. Other friends are like flowers in bloom, sharing giggles and the sheer exhilaration of joy. We may not see them often, but when we do, we leave with their fragrance on our hearts.

Evergreens. There may be one or two evergreens in the background of our stories, standing ready to provide us protection or shade. They are our mentors, who give by listening and offering us words of wisdom.

And then there are the everyday friendships—the kind that are more like art.

Everyday Friendships

It's how C. S. Lewis describes friendship:

> Friendship is unnecessary . . . like art. It has no survival value;
> rather it is one of those things that give value to survival.
>
> C. S. Lewis, *The Four Loves*

These are friends who hold on to our dreams the way a stream carries spring waters. They speak gently when we are running dry. They laugh with us when joy rises high.

The thing about friendship is this: it can be painful to see an everyday friendship go. But we cannot stop risking. Just as our souls can never grow tired hoping for sunsets, shooting stars, flowers in bloom, or art that moves us, we cannot give up on friendship.

Jesus stands by us, as our forever friend, always faithful to share beauty with us.

> I have called you friends. . . . You did not choose me,
> but I chose you.
>
> John 15:15–16 NIV

When we open up to friendship, we connect with Jesus through our hearts. We are saying, *I see beauty*, to another.

Josh got quiet, so I reached out to hold his hand and said, "Sweetie, Jesus made flowers to remind us . . . some things are beautiful, no matter how long they last. He wants us to enjoy them while we can." I nestled my cheek close to his. "There will always be new flowers."

Later that week, Josh brought home flowers from school. "Look, Mommy!" he squealed. "You can put them in your vase!"

As I hugged him, I smiled into him.

Yes, son. I'll put them in some water right now.

> Encourage each other every day while you have the opportunity.
>
> Hebrews 3:13 GW

vulnerability

Jesus often calls us to risk. He asks us to be vulnerable,
to be authentic, so others can see Him in and through us.

Mary E. DeMuth, *Everything: What You Give
and What You Gain to Become Like Jesus*

when you wonder
if they'll like you

holley gerth

I looked at the four lovely faces around me and my tummy did a nervous little flutter. A few weeks ago I had met these women when I spoke to a crowd of over six thousand at the Premier National Rally. After finding out some of the ladies who attended actually live in my town, I asked them, "Why don't we meet up for real-life coffee?"

I ran late on the way to our get-together. I let my hair blow dry by leaving the windows in my car down. I tried to order a breakfast sandwich and was told, "Um, it's *eleven*." (I wanted to reply, "I promise I've been up for a while, I just like eggs," but I didn't have the guts.)

Then I sat down at the table, straightened my jewelry, and fidgeted a bit. Eventually I decided I'd better just come out with it, so I took a deep breath and confessed: "I'm afraid you won't like me as much close-up."

You see, it's easy to look good from a distance. Especially when you've had a chance to write out every word you're going to say. And someone has kindly and beautifully accessorized you. And the lights are pretty and the decorations are fabulous and it's all so wonderfully in place for you. *What if I disappointed these women when they met just plain ol' me?*

Of course my fears were unfounded. Everyone was gracious and kind and funny and lovely and didn't mind my windblown hair or messy heart. *Whew.*

As I drove home, I thought about how the worry I expressed is one we all seem to share as women in one way or another. We all feel more comfortable with a little distance between ourselves and those around us because we're afraid we won't be loved if we're seen close-up.

We might create that distance by saying "I'm fine" when we feel broken inside, holding on to our couch like it's a lifeboat every evening, working too much, drinking too much, anything that will make us feel like we can avoid others seeing us as we *really are.*

But that's not how we're made to live, friends. We need to walk off the stage, walk out the door, walk across the room, and spill what's really going on in our lives. We need people who can see our faces without makeup and our souls without scripts and our lives without the polish and practice.

Yes, there is a time for putting our "best" forward. But there are days for inviting people into our worst as well. And most of all, there are moments for sharing everything that's in between. In other words, plain ol' lovely, ordinary, extraordinary *you*.

Let's be brave together, girls. Let's love and be loved. From near. From far. From wherever we are. *Because we're always better together.*

Two are better than one.

Ecclesiastes 4:9

encouragement is a powerful thing

mary carver

walked quickly through the parking lot, pulling my wiggly four-year-old along, sweating, and praying I could make it to the car before the tears spilled out.

No such luck.

As I reached my car, I heard my friend holler out her window, "And just where do you think you're going? Hold on! I'll pull around."

And so she did. I opened the door for my kiddo and turned on the car and its blessedly cool air-conditioning while my friend parked next to me and waited for me to walk around to her. Before I even could finish saying "Hey . . ." the stupid tears were slipping past my oversized sunglasses and down my red cheeks.

I told her my story, sniffling and rolling my eyes and whisper-shouting so the kids wouldn't hear. Like a good friend, she agreed with my take on the situation and said the words every-one longs to hear in the midst of an angry cry: "You're right."

She didn't stop there, though. As she maneuvered her two little boys and newborn baby girl out of her van, she said, "You let me know what I can do. If you need me to babysit or host some playdates, I'll do it. I'll help you! I want to help."

Then, after I tied her baby wrap and waited for her boys to move away from my car, we laughed at our awkward parking lot dance. She said, "Oh, I wish this wasn't happening right

153

now. I know you want to leave." And I thought, *Oh, I'm so glad this is happening right now. What a blessing I would've missed if I'd already left.*

It was just a moment—and just a chance meeting, really. As my friend pulled into the parking lot, flustered with her own story, she had no idea that I was speed-walking to my car, overwhelmed with mine. But she knew, when she saw me, that I needed some encouragement. And despite the three kids in her car and her own frustrations and worries, she took a few minutes to listen, to hug, to care.

And it meant a lot to me, that caring, that friendship, that encouragement. Because encouragement is a powerful thing. Whether someone has died, moved, gotten a new job, suffered a disappointment, gotten engaged, or just found out that she accidentally enrolled her daughter in the wrong preschool class, a kind word goes such a long way.

I felt it shelter to speak to you.

Emily Dickinson,
"Letter to T. W. Higginson,
January 19, 1878"

because friendship is a gift
deidra riggs

J knew I'd regret it the moment it happened. Or, to be more precise, the moment it *didn't* happen.

Last year, during Lent, I sat on a pew near the back of the sanctuary in a church in town. The back doors were open and the sun cast long shadows along the floor. A soft breeze danced just inside the doorway and I remembered that these weekly Lenten services had begun in the colder, darker days of winter. Michelle had welcomed me and we'd been riding together each week to sing the songs, eat the bread, drink the wine, pray the prayers, and listen to the messages in the days of preparation leading up to Easter.

On this night, our friend Lyla joined us and I sat in the pew with Michelle on my right and Lyla on my left. Together, the three of us sang the songs, ate the bread, drank the wine, prayed the prayers, and listened to the message about just how much God loves us. I wanted to reach out and grab my friends' hands, but I didn't. I had an inner dialogue going on, with one voice arguing that I'd freak them out if I reached out and touched them in the middle of the church service, and another voice telling me I'd regret it if I didn't. Fear of freaking out my friends won, and I kept my hands in my lap.

Later, in the parking lot, I told them, "I almost reached out and grabbed your hands, but I didn't want to freak you out."

"You should have," they both told me. "It would have been fine."

Last month, my husband and I visited Europe. We walked down street after street, in city after city, and saw pairs of women walking arm-in-arm or hand-in-hand everywhere we looked. They walked closely and leaned in toward one another and it was clear their friendships were treasures. I was smitten and I said to my husband, "I'm going to do that when we get home. I'm going to walk arm-in-arm with my girlfriends."

Friendship is a gift. I have learned that the hard way. Finding someone who will talk you back from the edge, encourage you to follow your dream, stay up talking until three in the morning, eat ice cream with you—straight from the container—hear your darkest confessions without flinching, and keep showing up anyway? A gift. No, a treasure.

If you've got one good friend, you've got a treasure, that's for sure. If you've got more than one good friend, you have what I've heard called an "embarrassment of riches." I want my friends to know how much I love them. I want them to know they have saved my sanity on more than one occasion. I want them to know that sometimes my heart overflows with gratitude and love for them. So I'm turning a deaf ear to the voice that tells me I might just freak out my friends if I let them know how much they mean to me. A friend loves at all times. It's as simple as that.

Touch is love made manifest, a way to connect not only human to human and skin to skin, but also with . . . that eternal, all-encompassing energy that unites us, that infuses us with life, that reminds us that we are indeed all one and that the world is a hospitable place to be. . . . Touching one another is what we humans do. Touch is what we need from one another and touch is what we have to give. It's what keeps us hopeful and what keeps us going, what keeps our hearts opening and softening and trusting.

Katrina Kenison, *Magical Journey*

more than meager graces

seth haines

Molly Beth and I sat in the hospital cafeteria; she was mashing macaroni and cheese under her plastic fork. "We had a baby chicken a few weeks ago," she said. "It got a foot disease or something so its momma kept pecking it to keep it away. It died." She said this matter-of-factly, like she was explaining the mechanics of a seesaw, or why all kids squish Jello through their teeth.

"You like that macaroni?" I asked, hoping to change the subject.

"Not as much as fruit snacks." She giggled and her cheeks pinked under her long blonde locks. She didn't catch the subject change. Molly Beth is still innocent. "You want a pink one?" she asked, sliding a star-shaped piece of goo across the table. "It'll make you feel better; it tastes like strawberries." She raised her eyebrows as she said "straw" and "berries," and her eyes opened wider, like blue full moons. Her gestures were emphatic, uninhibited.

Molly Beth's sister Suze, a diabetic, read my concern. At ten, Suze has become accustomed to the pin-pricking of life, the bloodletting. She checks her sugar with ritualistic precision. She understands the body's dependence on food. In some ways she is my youngest son's kindred spirit.

As we left the cafeteria, Suze reached for my hand. "Is Titus getting better?" she asked. Not sure how to answer, I squeezed her hand a little and stared farther down the hall. Feeling the awkward moment, Suze returned the hand squeeze. If I ever have a daughter I hope she'll be as intuitive. "Thank you for coming," I told Suze. She smiled.

Molly Beth moved to my open side, grabbed my left hand, and started swinging it like we were on the playground. The sisters skipped and for a moment I forgot why I was walking hospital halls.

The doctors have said that my son has failed to thrive. But these girls and their parents have come to bring solidarity. They've come to offer love, to lift my spirits.

Sometimes the dawn breaks backward and black, melting up from the horizon like tar. The stars flicker out, snuff silently under a rising tide. Sometimes the dawn breaks gray, hovering like a cloud of doubt. But even still there are light bearers that see through the most opaque. They know when gooey fruit snacks and a hand squeeze are more than meager graces. They know the innocence of mercy.

No one has ever become poor from giving.

Anne Frank, *The Diary of Anne Frank*

deep & wide

crystal stine

Making friends as an adult is much harder than I had anticipated. I always assumed by this stage in the game I would have mastered the art of small talk and would have this uncanny ability to attract new friends wherever I went.

I'm thirty years old (okay . . . thirty-one in April if we're being transparent) and I still struggle to find friends.

Twitter followers? Sure, those are easy.

Facebook friends I've never actually met in real life or interacted with . . . ever? Yep. Got 'em.

But I'm slowly discovering that God is calling me to do more than build a wide online community of readers, followers, friends, and fans. He's asking me to go *deeper*—and in real life—instead of wider.

For this introvert, that takes a lot of pretending to be braver than I am. Some days it might look like taking the time to pick up the phone and call a friend in my own town to meet for coffee.

Or making plans for a mini girls' day out to spend a few hours with a couple of other toddler mommas with a hot coffee and some leisurely perusing of the clearance racks at Old Navy.

Ultimately? It's taking the time to invest in someone else's life in a way that transcends screens and comment threads, and choosing conversations that hold more than 140 characters at a time. We are savoring time together.

I'm not very good at it, honestly. It's much easier for me to write to you from behind the buffer of this keyboard than it is for me to make eye contact with you in the grocery store

and feel confident that we might have something in common to talk about.

I'd rather send you an encouraging email than pick up the phone, and there is something about striking up a conversation with that other mom at the park that makes me feel like I'm the shy teenager with her nose always in a book to avoid social situations.

But I continue to be called to community, to the richness of life where we can reach out and touch the person beside us and watch their eyes twinkle as they laugh—literally—out loud.

In the speed of interacting online and in social media I discover that I've become so accustomed to quick responses that I've forgotten the art of conversation and how to really listen to someone.

So this year, I'm doing my best to step away from my comfort zone and into this space where community doesn't need to be big, but it does need to have depth.

This means looking at the two or three people God has put in my life and choosing to live authentically with them and watch the beauty of our messy, unedited, imperfect lives overlap one another.

You can't stay in your corner of the Forest waiting for others to come to you. You have to go to them sometimes.

A. A. Milne, *Winnie-the-Pooh*

what it really means to turn the other cheek

holley gerth

This world is not easy. People are imperfect. And we will get hurt. What do we do when that happens? I quietly asked that question in the dark of a worship service recently. I could still feel the sting of recent wounds from other women. (Yes, that kind of thing happens to me too.)

God, I whispered in my heart, *I know I need to love and forgive, but what does that really mean?* And this came to mind: "If anyone slaps you on the right cheek, turn to them the other cheek also" (Matt. 5:39 NIV).

When someone smacks you, the instant and unavoidable response is to turn away from them. They've forced you to do so. But what you do after that moment changes everything. *To turn the other cheek means you must turn back toward that other person.* You must look them in the eyes again.

Then you place yourself in a position of vulnerability by not only refusing to retaliate but also offering your other cheek. *Whew.*

Close your eyes for a moment and picture that. Someone smacks you. You turn back toward them and look at them with love. Then you choose to keep being vulnerable rather than becoming defensive. That's not how I want to respond in those moments. Instead I want to fight back or run away. But Jesus says to stand and stay. And not only that but to *love.* Love gets looked on as something soft in our culture. But I'm telling you, friend, love is fierce and strong and courageous. And there's no way I can love like that without Jesus.

I will not let my heart stay turned away from my sisters— even when I'm wounded. And I will never raise my sword against them. Instead I will use my words to fight the true enemy of all our hearts, every chance I get.

I walked out of that worship service with tears slipping down my cheeks. The cheeks that, with God's help, I was ready to turn toward others as many times as it took for love to win the battle.

PS: If you are in a physically abusive situation, that's a totally different scenario. Withdrawing from an abusive person until they show true change *is loving* because it stops a pattern that's destructive for them too. Please make sure you're safe.

But whosoever shall smite thee on thy right cheek, turn to him the other also.

Matthew 5:39

making a difference

No amount of kindness, no matter how small, is ever wasted.

Aesop, *The Lion and the Mouse*

leave room for yes

amanda williams

We're coming up. We leave tomorrow."

I tried to object but ended up crying and didn't bother trying again. The truth was, I was relieved. So very relieved. The truth was, I needed exactly what they were offering—not a task to be done, not a meal in the Crock-Pot, not another sincere "I'm sorry." I needed all of it at once. I needed them.

They were two of my very best life-friends and they still lived in the town where we went to college. They would leave their families the next morning to drive six hours north on a day's notice to do nothing other than carry my burdens. They were coming here to be *me*.

The eighteen months prior had been tremendously hard, and I'd never before been more aware of the separate and distinct life roles we all hold, the way they overlap and bump into each other in the course of everyday life. But the day before this phone call—the day my daddy's struggle ended and he went home for good—on that day the roles collided hard, loud and jarring like an interstate pileup. He was gone, really gone, and all four of me—the daughter, the sister, the wife, the mother—we all needed our room to grieve.

And so my friends arrived just as they said they would. They appeared at our door when the kids needed watching and disappeared when it was time to sleep. They'd made arrangements to stay with another friend in town so we wouldn't have to entertain, and they brought sandwiches to my mom's house on that awkward day in the middle, when the myriad of planning is done and all that's left is to say goodbye. They thought of everything and did it so quietly, so effortlessly, that it hardly allowed me any space for guilt, one of my go-to feelings in helpless situations.

There was a magic about this, come to think of it. They gracefully toed the line between asking and doing, not waiting for my permission yet allowing room for my yeses.

My two friends gave so much in those four days—the memory of it still fills my eyes with tears. They fed my little people and changed my twin boys' diapers. They swept my dusty floors and did my piled-up laundry. I'd not prepared for them at all, of course—cleaning house was not on the priority list in those last months—but they entered our mess as if they didn't notice, picking up where I left off and doing whatever needed to be done. They bought me feminine products, *for crying out loud*. They did it all just so I wouldn't have to.

It was love in action, love with no hope of payback.

When we decided it best not to take the littlest two to the burial, which required an overnight trip to East Tennessee, they made phone calls. They called their own husbands and checked in on their own small children—four between the two of them—and then stayed another night so we could go without worry.

For four days they filled in for me as mom so I could be fully present as daughter. It was an invaluable, unspeakable gift, and I will never forget.

People always ask what you need when you're grieving, but it's such an impossible question to answer. You need nothing and everything, you need companionship and space, you need room to feel all the joy and the anger and the sorrow and the stillness all at once.

Sometimes, in the worst times, you just need someone to be *you* so you can just *be*.

In the weeks that followed, we sent out the thank-you notes the funeral home gave us, the ones with Dad's name embossed on the front. I procrastinated sending theirs because, well, procrastination is what I do. But also, *how do you say thank-you for a blessing flung that wide?* I finally found some "Up a creek. . . . That's where I'd be without you" cards—because inserting humor into tense situations is also what I do—and I sent them with movie gift cards tucked inside. It was lame, but it was something. And I had to do something.

They entered the rawness of my grief and tackled the enormity of my need, and I sent them to the movies. It felt like that moment in the movie *Say Anything* when Lloyd

169

Dobler says blankly, "I gave her my heart, and she gave me a pen." But I knew they'd understand. Friends like those always understand.

Bear ye one another's burdens, and so fulfil the law of Christ.

Galatians 6:2

what you can do when life's storms hit

dawn camp

Churches, home-improvement and grocery stores, and perfect strangers housed stranded motorists last week as unexpected snow rocked the South. Hotels opened their lobbies when no vacancies remained. Truckers welcomed drivers into their cabs for warmth when cars, stalled for hours in traffic, ran out of gas. Teachers spent the night with students in schools when buses and parents couldn't get them home.

The insensitive or uninformed may mock us for the chaos that ensued from what seems like a modest amount of snow (and question why we and our local governments don't invest in equipment and supplies we rarely need for events like this), but then you'd miss the beauty that even snow and ice can't bury.

While Southerners may not have shown off their foul-weather driving skills, they certainly showed off their big hearts.

Tragedy breeds everyday heroes: the policeman who delivers a baby on a gridlocked interstate, the couple who leaves the warmth of home on foot to deliver food and water to the stranded, the principal who remains overnight and plays bingo with a handful of students who can't get home, families who welcome strangers into spare bedrooms for the night.

A crisis separates the well-intentioned from those who take action.

It doesn't take a snowstorm, a tornado, or a hurricane to find needs you can fill. My husband spent four days in the hospital last month. The day he came home, my friend Cindy sent me a text: "Dawn, I'd like to bring over a big pot of soup for y'all tonight if that would help." Did it ever! It was the nicest thing she could have done. I'd spent four days and nights sitting in the hospital with my husband and we all needed a home-cooked meal.

Recently Cindy's father had open-heart surgery and he didn't respond well to anesthesia or his medications. It's been rough on the whole family. When he leaves the hospital, he'll stay with my friend and her family for six weeks of recovery.

To Cindy—who's trying to take care of her daddy, her family, and direct a one-day-a-week private homeschool program—this probably feels like a seventeen-car pileup on I-285. Another friend coordinated a meal schedule and I had the opportunity to return Cindy's favor by delivering a pot of soup to her home.

Most people won't tell you what they need. Maybe they're too overwhelmed to think about it or maybe they don't want to impose on you, *even if you ask what you can do to help.* Just do something. Offer to take your friend a meal, to watch her kids, or to drive her to the hard appointments. Whatever she needs. Maybe you can be an everyday hero today.

If we would build a sure foundation in friendship, we must love our friends for their sakes rather than for our own.

Charlotte Brontë, as quoted in Elizabeth Gaskell,
The Life of Charlotte Brontë

how one small act can change someone's world

jennifer dukes lee

She wrote upside-down on the stationery, and she apologized for the mistake.

But in truth, her upside-down words were the most right-side-up words I had read in a long time.

Her name was Paula. She wrote me more than a decade ago, and her words covered both sides of her notecard. I found it while cleaning our filing cabinets the other day.

When I held it in my hands, one long rubber band of memory snapped me back to the day I got her note.

Two days before it arrived in the mailbox, Paula had visited my home. She and I sat together on the couch, with crushed Cheerios underfoot. I had drawn on lipstick before she came over, but Cover Girl couldn't cover the dark circles under my eyes. Nor could I hide the postpartum depression that had bulldozed my joy.

I had worn mismatched socks and tried to hide the wardrobe malfunction by pulling my legs under me. I sat on my feet until they tingled and went numb.

Paula was cradling my baby.

My husband and I had been attending Paula's church regularly, but for me, the liturgy and hymns felt like mouthed abstractions toward an unseen God. I was swimming through a soup of depression and drowning under the hot guilt of my puny faith in God.

For some reason, my doubt felt like failure, like something that needed to be confessed. Like something I should feel terribly sorry for.

So I kept my doubt walled off, and I nodded with the pastor when he preached the gospel, and I closed my eyes when I sang hymns, like maybe I could will myself to believe sometime before the organist hit the final chord.

The wall crumbled the day Paula came by.

She was old enough to be my mother. I didn't intend to unzip my heart that day. Maybe all of my bone-tiredness had loosened my steely resolve to keep secrets. I can't say for sure.

I do remember the softness of her eyes. The way she put her hands on my knees, like we were family. How she never swept away the crushed Cheerios with her feet. I remember, mostly, how my doubt came up and out, like it was busting out of a prison. Paula was like a parole officer.

And she was like a mother. I kept on talking, and she kept on loving.

A couple days afterward, her handwritten note arrived in the mailbox at the end of our country lane. I waited until I got back to the kitchen to read it, with my bare feet planted on the wood planks and a baby on my hip.

"Don't be discouraged by your doubting and empty feelings, Jennifer," she wrote. "Even after all these years, I feel empty at times."

A whole decade later, I sat in my office rereading those words through tears.

I had no idea, until all these years later, how important that note really was. And she would have had no idea how her small act of obedience—sitting down to write one notecard—would make a huge difference in the trajectory of one woman's faith life.

Before Paula, I had feared condemnation for my doubt. But she held it gently in her hands.

These days, I hear a lot about how the church is failing people. How it's too stodgy or irrelevant or happy-clappy or judgmental or legalistic or pick-your-favorite-adjective-and-insert-it-here. No doubt, the church has been one or all of those things for many people down through the ages.

But for me, on that day? Paula was church, the way church was intended to be, right in my living room and again in my mailbox. Because she rang a doorbell. Because she picked up a pen.

It didn't cost her more than the gas to drive to our house and the stamp on the envelope. And maybe a little time.

Mother Teresa, a giant in the faith, once told us all how the little things count for a lot: "Don't look for big things," she said. "Just do small things with great love."[1]

1. Mother Teresa, *Mother Teresa: Come Be My Light*, ed. Brian Kolodiejchuk (New York: Image, 2009), 34.

Small is the new big, which is good news for any of us who think that our small acts of obedience don't amount to a whole lot. Like Mother Teresa, Paula reminds us of this truth: it really is the little things.

You want to make a difference today? Go ahead, think small.

Send your kid's teacher a note of thanks. Bake cookies for your church janitor. Listen to the dreams of the woman who lives at the end of the cul-de-sac. Stop your car at the curb and help your elderly neighbor pick up sticks. Send the note, and don't fret if you write it on the card upside-down. Make the call. Pray your prayers. It matters. *It really matters.*

Look, you don't have to preach in stadiums or go viral or be a bestseller to radically alter the course of another human being's life. I've sat in many a conference-hall seat and have been wildly blessed by dozens of books and blog posts. But Paula's small act of love? *That* was the act that opened the door that let the light in. And if I wasn't writing about it right now, no one would ever know. It was done in secret. Out of love.

That's the power of small. It was a stepping stone.

After that meeting with Paula all those years ago, I found a way to pluck my bravery out from under my doubt. Later I became a leader in my church, even in the midst of my persistent questions about the faith. I began to teach Sunday school, to lead our church's Vacation Bible School program, and to serve as the "church DJ," spinning tunes from the church's music library on contemporary-worship Sundays. Later, I led community Bible studies, began a blog about my faith walk, and most recently wrote a book to encourage other Christian women who are also trying to figure things out.

You won't find Paula's name on the spine of any books, but she's built right into the spine of my faith story.

More than a decade ago, she wrote these words to me:

> Obviously, you are searching and studying and God is preparing you through that for what He has in store for you. Hang on—it could be a roller-coaster ride but with God in charge, you'll love it.

She added a postscript in the corner: "Sorry I wrote this upside down."

To be a Christian means to forgive the inexcusable because God has forgiven the inexcusable in you.

C. S. Lewis, *The Weight of Glory*

the momma code

shannon lowe

A few months ago, while out on a walk with my kids, I met a woman in our neighborhood who, it turned out, lived almost directly behind us. Kerry has two little boys; the youngest is only a couple of weeks older than my daughter Corrie. She and her husband had only moved to the area recently, and we were both glad to meet another mom in the neighborhood. We talked about schools and pediatricians and all the other stuff moms are required to discuss on their first meeting—then we traded phone numbers and went back to our respective houses.

I called Kerry a couple of weeks later to meet up for lunch at a Burger King with a play place. We had a nice—albeit *loud*—visit while our two-year-olds played. Actually, her two-year-old played; my two-year-old (who has three big brothers and therefore thinks that all human interaction involves fists) attempted to drop-kick, body-slam, and otherwise tackle my friend's little boy the entire time. I was mortified and apologetic and mumbled every few minutes about how she wasn't sleeping well lately, or some other lame excuse. Kerry was completely gracious, of course. We parted, and I hoped my new friend would want to get together again with That Strange Family Who Is Raising a Mean Girl.

The flurry of the holidays kept us from getting together, though our kids squealed at each other a few times from their respective backyard forts. Early this week, I was so pleased when Kerry called to invite us to her house for a playdate. I dressed Corrie in her frilly best (if she was going to *act* like a bully again, at least she wouldn't *look* like one), and we headed around the block for our second meeting with our new friends.

We arrived to find Kerry at the door, face white, on the phone with the doctor. Her older son had a bad fall in the garage moments before and immediately wanted to go to sleep—she was scared he had a concussion. She hung up and told me that the nurse said her son was fine as long as he didn't vomit, at which point he (of course) promptly vomited. I immediately offered to take her little one home with me so that she could take her son to the doctor, and I brought him back to my house with Corrie. As we pulled out of the driveway, Kerry looked at me, folded her hands, and mouthed the words *thank you* with a look of desperation. *No problem*, I mouthed back.

As I write this, Corrie and her little friend are playing happily in the next room (so far only one body-slam, I might add), and I've been praying for my new friend and her older son at the doctor's office. Our friendship consists of about

fifteen minutes' worth of conversation at this point, and yet we've both already had the chance to see each other at a particularly low moment. It's the reason, I believe, why "momma friendships" seem to be such deep ones, and why we bond so quickly. We're all on the same roller coaster, after all. It's as if there's an unspoken Momma Code that hangs in the air between us at all times: *this is hard please help me.*

In a society where asking for help is sometimes seen as a sign of weakness, motherhood forces us to reach out for others—it's simply too much for one person sometimes. It's the reason you watch a friend's child so she can take another

181

one to the doctor, because you know how hard that is. It's the reason you intercept a wandering toddler in the produce section, because the wild-eyed look of terror on the face of the mom two aisles away looks all too familiar. And it's the reason you take a meal to a friend who has morning sickness, because you've tried to fix a casserole between dashes to the bathroom. You do it with the assurance that you will likely be needing such kindness yourself soon.

So if things are smooth at your house today—if no one is sick or bleeding or fighting or grounded or has soccer/karate/dance/piano lessons—you can be *quite* sure that somewhere near you things are *not* smooth for another mom. Find her and *do something*.

And if you're the one up to your eyeballs, reach out and ask for help. Any mom worth her salt will sympathize and come to your rescue. She *has* to. It's part of the Code.

A friend may be waiting behind a stranger's face.

Maya Angelou, *Letter to My Daughter*

more patience

edie wadsworth

J was twenty-seven years old when I met her. *Susan Ward was the kindest, most gracious woman I have ever known.* Our sons went to school together and I had just graduated from medical school and was in residency training in family medicine. I was working eighty hours a week, sleep deprived, bearing a heavy weight of guilt because I was missing things like field trips and volunteering to work the lunch line at my children's school. I was short on sleep, short on patience, and short on friendship.

Susan had a smile a mile wide and the sweetest Mississippi accent. She introduced herself to me and invited my kids to play at her house after school. That was the beginning of a relationship that changed me and the way I have parented. I had never witnessed someone who was so patient and loving with her kids. She didn't see them as a distraction or a nuisance, and she was constantly teaching them and telling them stories.

I watched her every move: how she was so calm during her son's meltdowns and easily diffused the situation, how she talked so kindly to her boys when she corrected them, and how she constantly reinforced good behavior. She loved those boys and everybody knew it—most certainly them. I can't imagine how different my life would be if I hadn't met her.

I still work at that kind of love and grace and patience, especially with the kids.

Life is stressful and there are a hundred reasons to lose your cool every day. But when you see someone show mercy and grace and kindness and patience, *it stops you in your tracks*. It's not the normal way of the world. Susan's way of living and being with her family changed the trajectory of my life. It so inspired me that I began to reevaluate all of my relationships. Was I extending this kind of rare kindness, love, understanding, forgiveness, and patience to the people in my life?

I've spent a lifetime trying to grow up to be just like her.

The practice of patience toward one another, the over-looking of one another's defects, and the bearing of one another's burdens is the most elementary condition of all human and social activity in the family, in the professions, and in society.

Lawrence G. Lovasik, *The Hidden Power of Kindness*

find a safe place, be a safe place

dawn camp

I sit in a circle, head bowed, as three friends pray over me. Warm tears run down my face and I instinctively struggle to hold myself together, but I come undone and won't let go of these hands that grip mine. Why did I have to travel away from home to friends who usually smile at me from across a screen instead of across a table in order to come to this point, to feel the healing power radiating through this circle of women?

Because I haven't allowed myself a safe place.

No matter how put together we may look on the outside, we all experience dark times. Job loss. Illness. Struggling marriages. Broken dreams. Sometimes the problems aren't ours but belong to someone close to us, and we suffer for them.

We aren't made to handle these times alone. Our Lord is a present friend and a ready ear. Trust Him. But also seek a steady shoulder to cry on and a sympathetic friend to listen to you face-to-face.

For some this may come easily, but for others—like me—this level of vulnerability simply doesn't.

Find a Safe Place

Look for someone you trust who won't judge or gossip. Maybe a wise, older woman at church who's survived your stage of life and learned valuable lessons in the process. Maybe a long-distance friend with an outsider's perspective.

Just talk to someone.

Be a Safe Place

It would be easier if we wore signs around our necks, visible testimony to the struggles we face. But we don't. Sometimes we have to work to read each other's signs. When your girl-friend casually suggests a girls' night out this week, her calm tone may belie how desperately she needs some face-to-face girl time. Kind words and a sincere "How are you?" may provide the impetus for a much-needed conversation.

Be a safe place for friends who need to talk.

Who can you turn to? If you don't have an easy answer, make a conscious effort to identify a listening ear and a safe place for when you need it. Work to read the signs of personal struggle in those around you. This is friendship on its deepest level: find a safe place, be a safe place.

We are all in the same boat, in a stormy sea, and we owe each other a terrible loyalty.

G. K. Chesterton, *The Collected Works of G. K. Chesterton*, vol. 28

old friends

It takes a long time to grow an old friend.

John Leonard, as quoted
in Bernard Pierre Wolff,
Friends and Friends of Friends

traveling together

renee swope

From the beginning of time, God created us to be together in relationship—with Him and each other.

Designed in His image, we have a need for connection that comes from God, who has always been in community—Father, Son, and Holy Spirit.

My craving for closer friendships surfaced a few years ago while I sat across the table listening to and admiring the bond between two women I had just met during a luncheon. Their laughter was one of the most beautiful melodies I'd ever heard.

When I asked how long they'd been friends, they told me it had been more than sixty years. Sixty years. Although I was a little incredulous, the more time I spent with them the more obvious it became that, indeed, I was sitting in front of lifelong friends.

Admiring the way they loved each other, I noticed how well they knew each other and how much they enjoyed each other. When one paused, the other would finish her sentence and they'd both smile.

More interested in listening to their stories than eating my lunch, I put down my fork and picked up my pen like any good journalist and started asking as many questions as I could to find out their secret. How had they met? And what all had they done, all those years, to keep their hearts so closely knit together?

Their friendship started in grade school and continued long after they both married their high school sweethearts. Their husbands had played football on the same team, with a few others who were also still part of their "group," along with their wives.

They shared how intentional they had been to make their friendships last. And they made sure I knew it didn't just happen. Things had to be planned and time together had to be a priority. They vacationed together as families for years. And when they were young and had little money, they'd all get together to have a meal while the kids played. For years they had all met weekly to play cards, a tradition that was still going strong.

More than anything, they determined early on that they would be there for each other no matter what.

Now these two lifelong friends were widowed and counted on each other for companionship and laughter. They went on weekly shopping adventures and everything in between. They shared how they had an understanding that if one of them was feeling down she would call the other and say,

"Hey, I need to get out of the house," and they would go do something—together.

A friend who was with me shared how different our generation is, how busy we are. How much we rely on screen time more than face-to-face time. How much less our generation values building relationships and memories. Instead we're building stats, portfolios, and platforms.

A twinge of sadness came over me as I wondered whether there would be anyone in my life I would know for forty or fifty years, much less sixty years. Besides my husband, what friend will be able to finish my sentences when I am seventy or eighty years old? Who will know me better than I know myself?

This kind of friendship is a rare treasure. But if I want the wealth of real-life community and deep heart connections, I am the only one who can pray for it, look for it, and build it. But I am the worst about letting life get filled up with tasks that take up my time and leave me too tired to get together with friends.

Jesus's final prayer for His friends challenges me to change. In it I find His heart's desire is for us to be closely connected with each other, "that all of them may be one, Father, just as you are in me and I am in you" (John 17:21 NIV).

God did not create me to be a human *doing* but a human *being*, and part of that means being with my girlfriends. Even if it means getting together for lunch during our busy workday, meeting to plan menus for the week, doing laundry at one of our houses, cleaning out each other's closets, or running errands together. It's a start. Maybe a road trip to the beach or just going to the grocery store with a friend is all I need to start building a friendship that will last as long as I do!

You were all called to travel the same road and in the same direction, so stay together, both outwardly and inwardly.

Ephesians 4:4 Message

the glory of friendship
robin dance

It happened to me on Sunday.

We were visiting a new church where we knew no one, a very *large* church, one I had heard an old high school friend of mine *might* also attend. Actually, Thayer had been two grades ahead of me, the older sister of one of my best friends. We weren't close by any means, but I had spent many a night in their home and I looked up to her.

The fact that we were now living in the same town, several hours from our hometown, was reason enough for me to seek her out.

This was our third visit to the big, new church. Every visit, I kept my eyes peeled for someone who looked like my friend's big sister; it had been thirty years since I had last seen her, so I suppose I was looking for someone who looked like her mom.

It shouldn't have surprised me when I saw her, two rows in front of us, but it did. *Could that be her? Do I just walk up to her and introduce myself?* Could it be as simple as that?

When it was time in the service for those awkward moments of "greeting your neighbor," I shimmied out of our row and up to hers; I ran into her husband first and, testing the waters, flat out asked him his name. When he confirmed my suspicion, I blurted, "I'm a friend of your wife's from high school and she has no idea we're living here," and then I walked over to her.

She stared at me, smiling, that friendly greeting-a-stranger thing, and clearly she had no idea who I was. So I introduced myself. But before I could finish my sentence, recognition illuminated her face. She squealed, "You live here?!" and then

she threw her arms around my neck. I squealed with my indoor voice (or at least I hope I did).

Just like that.

Just like that!

Over three decades had passed since we last saw each other, but like a rubber band stretched across time and space, we snapped right back to Clarke Central High's glory days. It made little sense but it was precious.

That's the beauty of growing up in a small hometown, isn't it? You're connected by place and time, and years later something inexplicable still remains. Thayer and I weren't close but we shared life. And all these years later, affections linger.

Because I was brave enough to speak, to risk feeling silly or forgotten, I gained a lovely reward. It is a glory of friendship to be able to pick up right where you left off, no matter the time between visits. *No wonder we squealed.*

The heart always remembers what the mind tends to forget. Take a moment today to marvel at the ways you connect to others beyond time and geographical boundaries. What a treasure, a reason to celebrate, a wonder.

The pain of parting is nothing to the joy of meeting again.

Charles Dickens, *Nicholas Nickleby*

oh, friend

elizabeth w. marshall

I laugh when I think of
Running this race without you
This grace-laced life
Co-orbiting this spinning globe, linked arm in arm
The kind of laugh that is layered in double meaning
Like really, that could be done and would He have
    ever asked me to go it alone

And then I settle into the knowing that this is the way
    it is
Drenched in love
Wet with tears
Swimming in laughter
Split wide open with the knowing
That this was the way it would be
A you
And a me
An us

And a we
That we would trudge through real tragedy
Suffering would come and it would be heavy
Is there any other, friend

Yet in all the receiving
The glorious *once upon many a time*
Praying and seeking, longing and hoping
Never alone, but with a friend

In all the comfort that has been mine
In the tear wiping moments I've gathered and held
The mercy you've shown because you love Him

The whispering Truth and tough love
Always
Into my soul
Time and again

I think of the friendless
The ones without hope and I long to show Christ's
    love to them

Friendship is a sheltering tree.

Samuel Taylor Coleridge,
"Youth and Age"

what a friend

lynn d. morrissey

yrtle was dead. The shriveled brown body encasing her generous spirit let go at God's command. Like autumn's last leaf, thin and brittle as parchment, it drifted effortlessly to its final resting place.

I met Myrtle years ago. What an unlikely pair we were, our backgrounds and temperaments as variegated as fall's foliage. Myrtle was a venerable octogenarian of African-American descent—gracious, humble, and gentle. Yet her soft-spokenness was peppered with crisp humor and laughter that tinkled like a flurry of wind chimes. Her diminutive ninety-pound frame housed a prayer warrior who regularly conferred with her Captain and best friend, Jesus, whom she claimed could fix anything. And He did!

I was a thirty-something Caucasian with an impetuous nature. I loved God and His Word, but was frustrated by my faith that seemed to fluctuate like a round of "Simon

Says"—two baby steps forward, three giant steps back. Solidly standing with feet firmly fixed on her Rock, Jesus Christ, Myrtle's faith simply *was*.

I stuck close to Myrtle, hoping to absorb her faith secrets, and she was only too willing to share them. Every Sunday, we met in our church's tiny chapel. Myrtle always left the doors open so people could join us for prayer, but few ever did. Myrtle, whose arthritis might have dictated otherwise, insisted we kneel at the altar rail. Inch by inch, she pleated like a weathered accordion, and with one heavy sigh—*shooo*—would finally drop to her knees. I preferred my comfortable pew seat, but knelt out of respect for Myrtle. She knelt out of respect for God.

Myrtle prayed like she talked, simply and sincerely. I, who had struggled with prayer for nearly ten years as a Christian, was amazed at the effortlessness of her petitions, as if she were chatting over the breakfast table with an intimate friend. One knew that when Myrtle prayed, Jesus knelt alongside us, His presence palpable.

Myrtle didn't just pray to Jesus, she sang to Him too. Her favorite hymn was "What a Friend We Have in Jesus," and that was no surprise. She sang to her friend Jesus while she baked, washed, dusted, or tended the generational dozens of children entrusted to her care over the years. She told me that singing gave her spiritual strength. Myrtle sang most heartily in church, where she shone like a polished piano, ebony among mostly white keys.

Sometimes it disturbed me that Myrtle demonstrated what I considered to be a subservient attitude toward her Caucasian counterparts, calling each lady Miss or Missus. *Myrtle is just as good as they are*, I thought, *and knows her Bible better and can pray rings around them!*

In retrospect, although I believe Myrtle hailed from a generation plagued with societally imposed racial distinctions, I have learned that her personality was characterized by subservience to Christ. As His humble servant, she showed deference to others. *Her* humility humbled me, and I longed to be more like her.

What a friend I had in Myrtle. I called her day or night, asking endless questions or relaying uncontrolled fears. She patiently listened, never criticizing, never minimizing my wrestling. She'd offer a Bible passage to enlighten, a prayer to uplift. "Jesus will fix it, Lynn," she would assure me, and I would be soothed, though not always persuaded. My faith needed to grow.

Sometimes trials loomed larger than life, seemingly insurmountable. One morning at work I made a desperate call to Myrtle, explaining that some board directors thought I was negligent in raising critical funds for the agency for which I was executive director. Some wanted me fired. "Jesus will fix it," she insisted. "Let's pray." We did, and He did! I had never been one to toot my own horn, but at the next board meeting I had an opportunity to explain that I had personally been responsible for generating a large percentage of support in both cash and in-kind donations. A naive young woman, I had done my job without reporting it. In response to Myrtle's prayer, the Lord gave me courage to speak, and He gave me favor with the board.

Another call to Myrtle was even more desperate. I was forty and pregnant. This was a circumstance that couldn't

be fixed or altered by any amount of praying. And yet, in the ensuing months, as I confessed my anguish to my faithful, nonjudgmental friend Myrtle, Jesus answered our prayers by *fixing* my attitude. When our daughter was born, how proud I was to be her mother. And how proud Myrtle was to be included at Sheridan's christening as her great-godmother.

Certainly arrogant pride was not one of Myrtle's characteristics. "Why would you, a college graduate, ask advice from me?" she sometimes queried. I thought the answer was obvious. Myrtle possessed the God-given wisdom that I needed.

Yet near the end of her life, Myrtle's wisdom was harder to discover. Her quick mind and quicker wit were overshadowed by the ravages of Alzheimer's disease, scrambling her language into a kind of verbal Morse-code gibberish. She could no longer talk to others or to Jesus.

One afternoon, in what was to be our last visit, I pulled her dusty hymnal from the piano bench and asked her daughter-in-law for permission to play for Myrtle. As I played the old familiar hymn, with tears streaming down her cheeks, Myrtle began to sing, "What a friend we have in Jesus." Although she could no longer talk to Jesus, she was singing to Him just as she had throughout the years. While Myrtle couldn't tell Him, she knew He was still her best friend.

Several days later, Jesus fixed Myrtle good as new. And now she'll never stop singing.

> You can trust us to stick to you through thick and thin—to the bitter end. And you can trust us to keep any secret of yours—closer than you yourself keep it. But you cannot trust us to let you face trouble alone, and go off without a word. We are your friends.
>
> J. R. R. Tolkien, *The Fellowship of the Ring*

my mother, my friend

dawn camp

*I*n many ways I had an idyllic childhood. Grandparents, aunts, and cousins lived within two miles of our home. In summer I played baseball in my grandparents' yard, barefoot, where long balls landed among the furrowed rows of the garden. In autumn I gathered pecans, which our family valued as gold, as they fell from a tree whose limbs dangled over a sleepy side street, my daddy sailing a football high into the branches to knock them loose. Winter meant the gritty sweetness of Grandmother's snow ice cream if we were lucky enough to get it. The snow, that is. Spring brought softball season, a family affair: my daddy and Pappy coached my team, while my mother, who didn't have an athletic bone in her body, kept an immaculate scorebook.

My life was filled with family, *and family is good*.

I didn't realize how quirky my mom was until after she was gone. She was my mother, after all, the only one I'd known.

A lover of pastel colors, spun glass pianos, and "Made in Occupied Japan" china figurines, she was as fragile and feminine as the delicate things she collected, and yet she disdained "women's things." She thought we acted silly at wedding and baby showers and had no desire to play foolish games. She preferred to talk theology or politics.

Mother was also a rabid Braves fan and kept score in an actual scorebook—just like when I played ball—to stay calm during stressful games. A few months before she passed away, she told my aunt that she'd never made a pie or a cake and she was proud of it. I don't know how anyone, man or woman, lives to be fifty-eight years old without making a pie or a cake, but she managed it. That certainly didn't mean she didn't have a sweet tooth, though; if you are what you eat, my mom was a Little Debbie.

I don't remember having an attitude about my mom—in my mind my parents were always pretty cool—but I must have given her grief as a teen. As the mother of four daughters, two in their teens, I know my own girls think I'm clueless and out of touch. But by the time I reached adulthood, my mother had become my best friend.

My girlfriends watched each other's kids during pediatrician appointments and prenatal visits, and their friendships strengthened based on a system of mutual reliance. But I had my mother, *and ours was the friendship that bloomed.* Her health was poor, which limited her activities, but we did things together and talked on the phone every day.

She watched out for me in our dead-broke early married days, and I made sure she didn't overexert herself. She used to say, "Don't try to be something you're not." When she said it to me, it meant I should not get sucked into doing something I couldn't afford to do, just because everyone else was doing it. For her, it meant not trying to be a "healthy person," and not putting herself in situations she couldn't physically handle, like walking through a mall or going somewhere with stairs.

Some of us will do anything to not be like our mothers, even if it means making foolish decisions. My mom left me with valuable lessons I still learn from today. She passed from this world long before my need for her did. I'm thankful that I loved and appreciated her, and that we were the best of friends.

A mother is your first friend, your best friend, your forever friend.

Author unknown

contributors

Karina Allen is a freelance writer and editor who spends much of her days at the gym and her local church. She wrestles with calling and purpose through writing and community. She shares God's Word in a practical, conversational style at forhisnameandhisrenown.wordpress.com.

Tina Anderson is an artist, photographer, and writer. She writes about the joys and challenges of late-in-life motherhood and other random things at Antique Mommy, where life is sometimes sweet and sometimes tart, but always real.

Lisa-Jo Baker is the author of *Surprised by Motherhood: Everything I Never Expected about Being a Mom*. Her writings on motherhood are syndicated from New Zealand to New York, and you can catch up with her daily chaos at LisaJoBaker.com.

Dawn Camp is an Atlanta-based writer, wife, mother of eight, and editor and photographer of *The Beauty of Grace*. She lives with a camera in one hand and a glass of sweet tea in the other; blogs about family, faith, and Photoshop at MyHomeSweetHomeOnline.net; and also contributes to (in)courage.

Mary Carver is a writer, speaker, wife, mom—and recovering perfectionist. She lives for good books, spicy queso, and television marathons, but she lives because of God's grace. Mary writes about her imperfect life with humor and honesty at www.givinguponperfect.com. She is the coauthor of *Choose Joy: The Decision That Changes Everything*.

Sandy Coughlin is a full-time blogger and recipe developer, a wife, and the mom of three adult kids. She enjoys throwing parties, gardening, traveling, sharing about hospitality, connecting people, and bringing them together for memorable dinner parties. Sandy blogs at ReluctantEntertainer.com.

Married to her college sweetheart and mom to three, **Robin Dance** dreams of Neverland and Narnia. She's a ragamuffin princess and as Southern as sugar-shocked tea. She's sometimes lost, sometimes found, and always celebrates redemptive purpose at robindance.me.

Sarah Forgrave is a novelist whose work has been featured in Guideposts Books and the webzine *Ungrind*. In her spare time, she teaches fitness classes and stays busy keeping up with her energetic husband and two kids. To learn more, visit www.sarahforgrave.com.

Joy Forney is the wife of a missionary pilot and momma to five. Living abroad brings her to the foot of the cross time and time again, and no matter her geographical location, she still finds God faithful. She blogs about her adventure of a life at joyforney.org.

Holley Gerth is a bestselling author of several books, a life coach, and a speaker. She also cofounded the website (in) courage and blogs at www.holleygerth.com.

Bonnie Gray is the author of *Finding Spiritual Whitespace: Awakening Your Soul to Rest* and the inspirational speaker and soulful writer behind FaithBarista.com, serving up shots of faith for everyday life. She is featured on DaySpring's (in) courage and in *Relevant* magazine, and her writing is syndicated on Crosswalk.com. Bonnie lives in Northern California with her husband, Eric, and their two sons.

Alia Joy Hagenbach is a storyteller, speaker, and homeschooling mother of three. She shares her story in broken bits and pieces on her blog Aliajoy.com, and finds community where others' stories intersect. She's also a regular contributor at Allume, SheLoves, and (in)courage.

Seth Haines is a working stiff who makes his home in the Ozark mountains. He and his wife, Amber Haines, have four boys and a dog named Lucy. Seth enjoys music, food, fly fishing, and fine sentences. He is the author of *Coming Clean* (Zondervan, 2015), a story of pain, faith, and the abiding love of God. You can find him at sethhaines.com or on Twitter @sethhaines.

Liz Curtis Higgs is the author of more than thirty books with 4.5 million copies in print, including her bestselling *Bad Girls of the Bible*. Her messages are biblical, encouraging, down-to-earth, and profoundly funny. Liz has one goal: to help women embrace the grace of God with joy and abandon.

Sophie Hudson loves to laugh more than just about anything. She is the author of *A Little Salty to Cut the Sweet* and *Home Is Where My People Are*. In addition to her blog, BooMama. net, Sophie is a contributor to the Pioneer Woman's blog and serves as co-emcee for LifeWay's dotMOM event. Sophie lives with her husband and son in Birmingham, Alabama.

Becky Keife is momma to three of the most spirited, dirt-loving little boys the Good Lord ever made. She's a passionate storyteller and loves encouraging women from an in-the-trenches perspective. She writes to slow time, give thanks, and awaken to God's daily wonders and grace at www.becky keife.com.

JoAnne Kelly enjoys writing as a hobby between her part-time job and playing with her two beautiful young grandchildren. She and her husband live in Toronto, Canada, with their black golden retriever, and love spending time with their four now-grown children whenever they can.

Jennifer Dukes Lee is a grace dweller and storyteller at www .JenniferDukesLee.com. She and her husband live on the family farm in Iowa with their two girls. Jennifer is the author of *Love Idol: Letting Go of Your Need for Approval—and Seeing Yourself through God's Eyes*. She is a community editor for TheHighCalling.org and a monthly contributor for Dayspring's (in)courage.

Lisa Leonard creates jewelry out of her California workshop. She and her husband have two sons, one with special needs. Their story of finding beauty in brokenness is woven through every product they create and through her blog, LisaLeonard. com.

Shannon Lowe blogged for many years at www.rocksinmy dryer.typepad.com. Her writing has appeared in numerous books and magazines, including *Good Housekeeping*, *Parenting*, and *Chicken Soup for the New Mom's Soul*. She lives in Oklahoma with her husband and four kids.

An introverted extrovert, **Elizabeth W. Marshall** is a *curious noticer* who lives by the sea in a small Southern shrimping village. She and her husband are lovingly renovating a historic house built in 1904. Because of Elizabeth's love for all things French and as a hat tip to her gratitude, she has named her new old home Mersea. Visit her at her writing home, elizabeth wmarshall.com, where she sees the world through a lens of grace. Most days she can be found staring out the window, looking for beauty, and writing poetry. Married for twenty-six years, she is the momma of three growing-up children. Find her on Twitter and Instagram @graceappears.

Melissa Michaels is the creator of the popular decorating blog The Inspired Room and the author of *Love the Home You Have*. She encourages over a half-million women each month to find beauty, contentment, and purpose in creating a home. Melissa is a church planter's wife and mom living in the beautiful Pacific Northwest.

Lynn D. Morrissey is the author of *Love Letters to God: Deeper Intimacy through Written Prayer* and other books, a contributor to numerous bestsellers, and a professional journal facilitator, speaker, and soloist. She's passionate about encouraging transparency in women through reflective journaling. Contact her at words@brick.net or on Facebook.

Tsh Oxenreider is the author of *Notes from a Blue Bike: The Art of Living Intentionally in a Chaotic World*. You can find her spearheading a community blog about simple living at The Art of Simple, or on Twitter @tsh.

Crystal Paine is a wife, mom of three, founder of MoneySaving Mom.com, and author of the *New York Times* bestseller *Say Goodbye to Survival Mode*.

Having lived in four countries, **Laura Parker** and her family now call Thailand home. She and her husband lead a nonprofit organization called The Exodus Road, which fights sex trafficking. She has published a book about their journey, *The Exodus Road*, and blogs at www.LauraParkerWrites .com.

Katie Kenny Phillips and her husband are raising their five children (three biological and two by way of foster care and adoption) in Atlanta, Georgia. She writes about the glory of when God shows up in the midst of a messy, hilarious, beautiful, obedient life at www.operationleapoffaith.com.

Sharing Jesus through the arts is **Melanie Porter**'s forte as she is a playwright, blogger, women's Bible teacher, and a Christian theatre team director. Always an optimist, Melanie is a wife and a sentimental, recovering helicopter mom to three big boys.

Christie Purifoy earned a PhD in English literature at the University of Chicago before trading the classroom for an old farmhouse and a garden. She lives in Pennsylvania with her husband and four children, where she observes the seasonal beauty of God's good creation. Her poetic reflections can be found at www.christiepurifoy.com.

Anna Rendell is the author of GirlWithBlog.com and a regular contributor to DaySpring's (in)courage. She is a seasoned speaker and presenter, formerly worked in youth and outdoor ministry, and now works from home as the social media coordinator for incourage.me. Anna is married to Jared, is mother of a toddler boy and a baby girl, and lives in Minnesota.

Lesli Richards, mother of five, is coauthor of the award-winning *Homegrown Preschooler* and the newly released *A Year of Playing Skillfully*, a play-based developmental preschool curriculum. She enjoys sharing her passion for classical education and building wonder in children with parents across the country.

Deidra Riggs, a writer and speaker, claims an undying devotion to disco music, the Motor City, and long bike rides under a big, blue sky. She is managing editor at The High Calling and a monthly contributor to (in)courage. As founder of

Jumping Tandem, Deidra inspires individuals to join God in the adventure He has uniquely designed for them. Deidra and her husband live in Lincoln, Nebraska. They are the proud parents of two adult children and happy inhabitants of an empty nest. Deidra's first book is *Every Little Thing: Making a World of Difference Right Where You Are* (Baker Books, 2015).

Ruth Chou Simons is an unlikely mom to six young boys and wife to a very patient man. Online, she's an artist, writer, and speaker who shares her journey and how God's grace intersects daily life at her blog and shop, GraceLaced.com. In her everyday life, she washes eight loads of laundry a week, cooks for large crowds, and educates her children from home part-time through the classical Christian school she and her husband, Troy, founded in Albuquerque, New Mexico.

Myquillyn Smith, "The Nester," encourages women to embrace the home they are in. After moving thirteen times in eighteen years of marriage, she, her husband, and three boys now live on twelve acres in North Carolina where they're renovating a neglected farm and host events at The Barn, a retreat space. She is the author of *Nesting Place: It Doesn't Have to Be Perfect to Be Beautiful.* Follow her blog at www.thenester.com.

Crystal Stine is passionate about living authentically, chasing joy, and encouraging women to savor the season God has them in. She works full-time as the editorial and marketing manager at (in)courage and shares daily encouragement at her blog, crystalstine.me.

Kristen Strong is wife to a retired Air Force veteran and mom to twin sons and a daughter. She is the author of *Girl Meets Change: Truths to Carry You Through Life's Transitions.* She lives in the Rocky Mountain country of Colorado and writes of the fresh-air hope found in Jesus at her blog chasing blueskies.net.

Ann Swindell is a writer, wife, and momma who is passionate about seeing her generation set ablaze with the love of Christ. She writes about marriage, motherhood, and God's presence in daily life at www.annswindell.com.

Renee Swope is a Word-lover, heart-encourager, story-teller, and grace-needer. She's also the bestselling and award-winning author of *A Confident Heart* and cohost of Proverbs 31 Ministries' radio program. Renee writes for *Encouragement for Today* devotions and (in)courage, and loves connecting with women online at www.ReneeSwope.com.

Lysa TerKeurst is the *New York Times* bestselling author of *The Best Yes*, *Unglued*, and *Made to Crave*. She is president of Proverbs 31 Ministries and writes from her sticky farm table in North Carolina where she lives with her husband, Art, five kids, three dogs, and a mouse that refuses to leave her kitchen. Connect with her at www.LysaTerKeurst.com.

Jessica Turner is the founder of the popular lifestyle blog The Mom Creative and author of *The Fringe Hours*. Additionally, Jessica is an (in)courage writer, World Vision blogger, and cohost of the Bloom Book Club. She and her family live in Nashville, Tennessee.

Edie Wadsworth is a momma, writer, blogger, foodie, cowboy boot–wearer, and hospitality fiend. She's a lover of truth, beauty, and goodness and seeks to inspire women in their love and service of others at the lifestyle blog www.lifein graceblog.com.

Amanda Williams is a writer in love with honest words and the way they make us feel less alone. She lives in a loud farmhouse outside Nashville, Tennessee, with her husband, David, and their three children.

Francie Winslow lives in the Washington, DC, area with her husband and four kids. Francie's passion is to see women and families made whole in Christ. Specifically, she speaks and writes on the power of married sex to equip couples for abundant life in God's kingdom. Find her at franciewinslow.com.

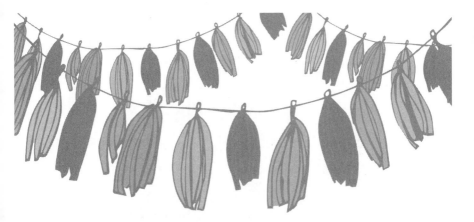

Get to know

Dawn Camp

Read her blog

&

Join the conversation

MyHomeSweetHomeOnline.net

also available from

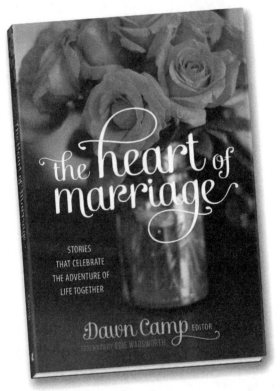

Collecting true stories from some of today's best writers, Dawn
Camp invites you to reflect on the heart of marriage. With beautiful
photographs and poignant prose, this collection is perfect for the
good days, the hard days, and all the days in between.

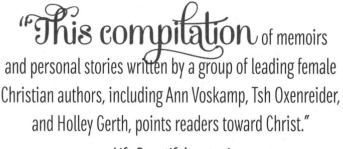

"*This compilation* of memoirs and personal stories written by a group of leading female Christian authors, including Ann Voskamp, Tsh Oxenreider, and Holley Gerth, points readers toward Christ."

—*Life:Beautiful* magazine

FOREWORD BY
HOLLEY GERTH

the beauty
of grace

stories of God's love

from today's most popular writers

Dawn Camp EDITOR & PHOTOGRAPHER

Revell
a division of Baker Publishing Group
www.RevellBooks.com

Available wherever books and ebooks are sold.

Learn to
Make Time for Yourself and Thrive through Change

CELEBRATE the Value of Rest, Faith, and Community

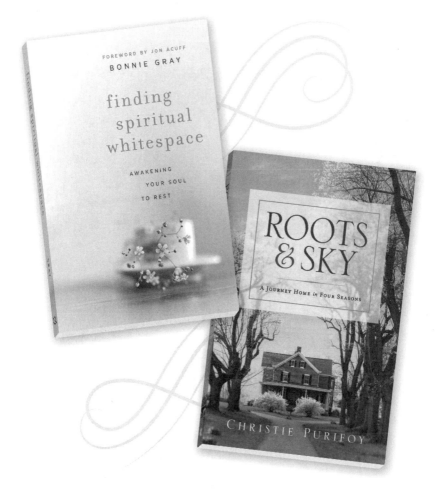

Perfect Companions for the
Wall Street Journal Bestselling Book